Pages of Enchantment

A Journey Lost in a Book

Payal Shah

Chennai • Bangalore

CLEVER FOX PUBLISHING
Chennai, India

Published by CLEVER FOX PUBLISHING 2023
Copyright © Payal Shah 2023

All Rights Reserved.
ISBN: 978-93-56489-62-2

This book has been published with all reasonable efforts taken to make the material error-free after the consent of the author. No part of this book shall be used, reproduced in any manner whatsoever without written permission from the author, except in the case of brief quotations embodied in critical articles and reviews.

The Author of this book is solely responsible and liable for its content including but not limited to the views, representations, descriptions, statements, information, opinions and references ["Content"]. The Content of this book shall not constitute or be construed or deemed to reflect the opinion or expression of the Publisher or Editor. Neither the Publisher nor Editor endorse or approve the Content of this book or guarantee the reliability, accuracy or completeness of the Content published herein and do not make any representations or warranties of any kind, express or implied, including but not limited to the implied warranties of merchantability, fitness for a particular purpose. The Publisher and Editor shall not be liable whatsoever for any errors, omissions, whether such errors or omissions result from negligence, accident, or any other cause or claims for loss or damages of any kind, including without limitation, indirect or consequential loss or damage arising out of use, inability to use, or about the reliability, accuracy or sufficiency of the information contained in this book.

Preface

I must share that I've been a Disney fan for as long as I can remember, not just of Disney movies but also of any fantasy stories or films. I've always admired how these stories could transport us to another world through sheer imagination. There was a time when I couldn't wait for a good fiction movie to sweep me off my feet. Sometimes, I even found myself craving more after watching one, which led me to start imagining and creating stories in my head that I wished I could watch on screen.

I was so deeply immersed in this world of imagination that even my dreams started following similar patterns. "Pages of Enchantment" is the result of those imaginative journeys. I began crafting this story during my high school years. As a teenager, I reveled in daydreaming, which eventually evolved into a written narrative. This story holds a special place in my heart because it's the first among those countless imaginings that I managed to put into words.

However, as much as I enjoyed imagining and writing it, I was always hesitant to share it with the world. I lacked confidence in whether people would appreciate it. With the passage of time, life took its course, studies took precedence, followed by a job and then marriage. There always seemed to be something more urgent, and my fantasy world took a back seat.

But one day, I made the decision to finally publish it. It took me over a decade to summon the courage to release this story to the public, to give it—and myself—a chance that I should have taken long ago. I always knew that there were countless great stories out there, and I was uncertain if my story could measure up to any of them. Over time, I often wondered how it would fare or if people would even enjoy it if it were ever published.

Nevertheless, better late than never, here it is—my whimsical teenage imagination. I hope you enjoy it.

Contents

PAGES OF ENCHANTMENT v
1. The Book 1
2. Where is Doris? 11
3. The New Place 17
4. The Guy 26
5. An Attack 36
6. Back to Her 44
7. The Prince 61
8. I Hate Kids 65
9. An Argument 84
10. An Invitation 96
11. Christine's Secret 113
12. I Know the Story 126
13. Reality Hit 146
14. Personality Change 154
15. A Tragedy 161
16. The Conspiracy 171
17. The Surprise 188
18. She Is a Witch 194

Contents

19. The Dungeon 212
20. The Lost Princess 221
21. The Celebration 232
22. The Curse 243
23. Back to Reality 257
24. The Goodbye 263
25. Back Home 270
26. Sweet Memories 275
27. The Happy Ending 283

PAGES OF ENCHANTMENT

Chapter 1

The Book

*H*igh school is a place that gives us the most memorable moments of our lives. It is the place where we live more in our daydreams than we do in reality. The time when we are still trying to figure out what life is about and how to love it. Everybody wants something magical or extraordinary to happen in their lives deep inside, even though some of them do not like to admit it. For some, it really is heaven, but it can be hell too.

Well, it all depends on how we deal with situations and ourselves. And just as in almost every high school, where rich brats exist to make other people's lives miserable, the high school from this story too has Doris and her clique who were as fun-oriented, sometimes at the expense of others and their own future, as one can imagine.

Skipping classes, having fun, bothering others—or you could say *bullying*—having arguments, and spending days out were almost routine for her and her friends, Kate and Cyril. As a beauty, Doris was out of every boy's league in her school. Many tried to date her, but you could say they could not stay.

Her teachers and other students were deeply annoyed with her but could not speak much against her because her parents were high-profile people and members of the high school management committee. Her mother, Rachel Wilson, was quite particular about her and discipline though. But Doris, clever as she was, always made sure complaints never reached home.

One day, Doris and her friends skipped classes and went to the private beach Doris's father, Richard Wilson owned, for fun. Since their summer break was just over, the beach was not quite crowded. Even though the beach was for members only, it was still busy in the season and famous in the area. Doris, as the daughter of the owner, had quite a reputation there and had the employees under control. They obeyed her when she told them not to inform her parents about her skipping classes and being on the beach instead, to keep their lives easy going.

As they had this visit planned already, they had all the required things with them. Just as they liked and did almost every year. They swam, surfed, and played volleyball. In the end, they lay down on sun loungers to bask under the afternoon sun.

Doris, after some time, saw a little girl making a sandcastle nearby. Suddenly, she felt the urge to make a sandcastle too.

"I'm bored," she said to her friends.

"Bored? I am having a good time relaxing after playing volleyball for so long," Kate said, with her eyes closed under the sun covered by her hat.

The Book

"Well, I'm going to make a sandcastle. Any of you losers wanna join?" Doris asked.

"You must be kidding, right? What are we? Some 10-year-olds?" asked Cyril.

"I feel like making one. Thought I'd ask in case you want to join, or whatever," Doris said, getting up to do what she made up her mind about.

She asked for sandcastle tools from a passing by beach waiter who managed to get her what she wanted on priority.

"What? She wasn't kidding?" Cyril asked, confused.

Kate opened her eyes and saw Doris putting her hands in the sand, trying to make something out of it.

"Oh dear, I don't understand her sometimes," Kate said, getting up from her place too.

"You are going too?" Cyril asked, but Kate left, ignoring his question. "Oh boy, Jack was right! They are gonna turn me into a girl one day." Cyril got up to join them as well.

Doris was digging some sand out for the castle when suddenly her trowel struck something hard. She removed the sand with her bare hands and found a small wooden box. It was all wet and partially decayed for obvious reasons.

"Hey, look what I found in here!" Doris said with excitement to Kate.

When they both opened it, they found an ancient-looking book that fit perfectly in the box. The book had hard metallic binding with golden plates at the corners and was blood red in color. Doris struggled to take it out of the box.

"Since when did you start taking an interest in books?" Cyril exclaimed, seeing a book in Doris's hands and walking toward her.

"I have no interest in books … and it's not mine. I found it here," she explained with an annoyed expression, still struggling to get the book out of the box.

"It seems to be somebody's diary. Let's see if something's written in it!" Kate said with excitement when the book finally came out.

"I will only be interested in it if we find a treasure map here." Cyril was betting by his judgments, looking at such a regal-looking book found in the sand.

Doris opened and found nothing written on its pale-yellow pages. Besides, they were wet.

"See … there is nothing to be so curious about," Doris said.

"It looks very old. It seems the words inscribed have been erased over time," Kate replied.

"Oh, forget it! We are talking as if we got a treasure map. What do we have to do with this dumb old book anyway? Can't believe I touched this rotten crap." Doris threw the book behind her.

As she picked up her handbag, the book suddenly opened on its own, and a greenish light emanated from it with a voice calling for help. Cyril saw that and shouted anxiously, "Hey! What the hell is that?"

All three were astonished.

As they walked closer to it, Doris hesitated, tried holding the book to look in, and opened it. But suddenly, she felt like she was being pulled into it and, in no time, was engulfed by the greenish light. It was as if she just entered the book. The book closed itself and fell on the sand, while Doris's scream faded and became inaudible.

Cyril and Kate could do nothing but just stand and watch in bafflement as it all happened quickly and unexpectedly. They did not even get time to scream or ask for help.

Doris had suddenly just disappeared right in front of their eyes into the book!

"What the hell just happened!" Cyril screamed.

"Doris! Doris!" they both cried.

They searched around for her but could not find Doris. Only the book and the box were still there, which were of no use and provided no clues. Both were frightened and very confused. They waited there for her until dusk. Nevertheless, Doris did not reappear. As they walked back with heavy hearts, they tried to think of what they'd tell Doris's parents on the way. After a very long discussion, they decided to tell them exactly what had happened.

They reached her house and rang the doorbell, bringing the box along. Doris's mom opened the door. The look on her face said that she was furious. "Now, where the hell is she? And by the way, may I know where the hell the three of you have been the whole day today?" Doris's mother asked them while her eyes were seeking her daughter.

However, both of them had no words to say and, therefore, stood quietly in front of her.

"Come on … tell me now. I called your physics teacher half an hour ago, and guess what I got to know from there?" she asked, knowing it herself, and continued without pausing, "I heard that you guys were absent the entire day from the school! Your mischief and complaints are increasing each day. Tell me where she is, or else, I am telling your parents too. And Doris … she is so grounded," Doris's mother questioned them about her again.

"We will tell you all about Doris, but *you must believe us*," Kate said, feeling all frightened.

"Believe? You two? Yeah, right!" Doris's mother replied.

"What? What do you mean?" Cyril asked in confusion.

"I mean I cannot trust you. What did you think?" Doris's mother said in anger.

"Oh … oh, you were talking about trust!" Cyril muttered with a wry smile.

Kate stared at him. He went quiet again, looking as if someone beat him up.

"Mrs. Wilson, please *try* to understand what we want to say," Kate continued after pausing for a minute while Mrs. Wilson was curious to hear their new excuse. "She is lost. Doris is lost!"

"Yay! Finally … thank you, God!" George, who was coming downstairs from his room, heard what Kate said, and exclaimed with joy.

George was about four years younger than his elder sister Doris.

"Seriously? You have *these* kinds of thoughts for your sister? You should be ashamed," his mother rebuked him.

"Who wouldn't want to get rid of her?" George mumbled, softly rolling his eyes.

"Go back to your room, George." His mother fumed at him. Then, turning toward the two of them, she carried on, "And what rubbish! Is she a small kid to be lost somewhere? I know that she must have realized that she would be grounded after the complaints about her. That is why she has set this up. She might be a genius at making excuses, but I am her mother, you see. Let her come home. Where would she go anyway? She must come back here."

"What happened? What is the fuss about?" Doris's father came out of his room.

"*What happened?* You and your dear little daughter will turn me crazy one day. Doris, she has not returned home. Instead, her friends have come over here with a wonderful made-up story. She skipped her classes today too. Oh God! I don't understand what to do with this girl!" Doris's mother complained to her father, who walked into the living room and sat on a couch.

"So what? She is not a kid anymore. Why don't you sometimes let her enjoy her life? Can't you treat her like a grown-up now?" Doris's father tried to calm his wife down.

"All right, then. Do whatever you like," she said in frustration.

"Mrs. Wilson, *please* listen to us. We are not making any excuses about Doris. She *really* is lost," Kate said, walking inside.

Doris's father asked her friends completely worried, "She what? How? When? Where—"

"Oh please, don't fall into their trap," Doris's mother interrupted. "Call her. Call her now."

"We tried like a hundred times, but her phone is unreachable," said Cyril.

"Hear them out, Rachel. They might be speaking the truth. And this sounds something very serious." Doris's father wanted to hear them out.

"What happened exactly?" Doris's father asked, worried.

"We don't know, Mr. Wilson. It will sound crazy to you. We are still trying to process this because what happened there was so unreal. We went to the beach instead of our classes …" Kate tried to articulate the incident in the best way possible.

Doris's mother looked at her father as if to say, "See, didn't I say so?"

"Look we accept our fault, but it led to something serious, so hear me out." Kate explained.

"I am listening…" Doris's father asked concerned.

The Book

"There, Doris found this ancient-looking book. She opened it to have a look, there was nothing written inside it. So, we threw it back, but then suddenly we heard someone crying out for help, so Doris picked it back and then suddenly disappeared into it. *Within this book!* I know this ... this sounds insane. It really doesn't even make any sense to me as I'm telling you ... but that is what happened. We waited for her till dusk, but she didn't come back!" Kate stammered to Doris's father, showing him the book as proof, which did not make any sense either.

Doris's father listened to them very patiently, but since it was unrealistic, he obviously did not believe their story.

"Hmm ... I think in this matter, Doris's mother is right. You people have just ruined my image. You should have thought about a better excuse at least! Do you know I used to be very smart at making excuses when I was your age? You need to make it sound more authentic, more realistic; you know." Mr. Wilson said with a disappointed smile.

"I wonder whom she has taken after," Doris's mother said, rolling her eyes.

"No, we are not making things up, Mr. Wilson. Please believe us. I was there too and saw all that happened. Kate is not lying," Cyril said to corroborate Kate's claim.

"You are freaking me out now. Seriously, where is Doris?" Doris's mother asked with concern now.

"We knew that you wouldn't believe us. But please ... I believe something terrible has happened to Doris. *Please take our words seriously*. Doris … Doris is gone!" Kate said with a cracked voice and wet eyes.

"Hey, are you really crying? You … you are not lying?" Doris's father suddenly appeared willing to give them a chance and turned serious about it.

"Oh, you believe us now?" Cyril sighed.

Then, they realized that something serious had happened. Kate and Cyril thought that Doris's parents finally believed their words, but it was not so. Mr. and Mrs. Wilson thought this was some foul play.

Chapter 2

Where is Doris?

Doris found herself in a strange place. She felt as if someone had thrown her there from a height. She was dazed while scanning the place and trying to stand up. She had never seen that place before in her life.

"Oh my God! Now, where am I? This isn't a dream for sure because my leg hurts," Doris cried while trying to walk a little.

Her hands ran through her hair as she tried to get hold of the situation. She was standing on a pedestal constructed in an abandoned and ruined structure. In fact, she felt there should have been some kind of statue where she was standing. Indeed, she found remnants of one scattered around her feet. She got down from there and tried to look for the face of the broken statute. However, to her dismay, it was damaged beyond recognition, though it seemed to have been of a woman.

"Kate? Cyril?" she shouted at the top of her voice. "Hello! If you guys are here too, please answer me. Kate? I am freaking out right now. Is somebody listening?"

No other human was visible around. Fallen pillars and walls were scattered on the ground. The complete premises did not cover a large area though. The overgrowth of the vegetation indicated that people seemed to have forgotten the place.

She walked around and found no other structures. The only structure was that from which she had come out. It seemed to be constructed to commemorate someone. It was amid a thick forest.

The mist was lowering from the treetops. Birds were flying back toward their nests to rest. Doris was still only in her swimsuit, and it was very cold around. One of her handbags was thankfully hanging around her shoulder. She searched through her bag but could not find any dry clothes.

"Damn it! This seems like some kind of nightmare!" She could not understand how all her clothes had gone wet. She held her hands across her body to avoid the cold a little.

"No clothes, no food. Hope I don't run into some wild animals. I must move out of here … quickly," Doris murmured to herself.

She covered a little distance and found a small brook. She followed it downstream. It seemed like it had been ages when, from a distance, she saw someone sitting by the brook. By her appearance, it seemed like a girl. She was happy to find a living soul at last. The girl was washing some utensils across the bank and seemed to be in her late teens, as Doris herself was. There was a single cottage alone, which looked from ages ago and was surrounded by wooden fencing separating it from the rest of the forest. The premises was without any modern construction. The girl was wearing some ancient clothes, somewhat like those of the medieval ages.

What is she wearing? Is this a movie set or something that I've walked into? But nobody is around. Going to a costume party perhaps, Doris thought, quickly scanning the place.

"Excuse me! Could you please tell me where I might be?" she asked the girl, approaching her from behind.

"You are in a forest, my dear," the girl answered Doris without looking at her busy in her chorus.

"Very funny. Now, seriously, could you please answer me straight? I am in trouble. I am lost, you see." This was the best way Doris could ask again in her helpless condition.

"Oh, I am truly sorry," the girl turned around to have a look and shouted with disbelief, "My goodness! Wha ... what on earth are you wearing? I mean, why are you not wearing anything? Where are all your clothes? Oh, you poor girl, have you been *robbed* in the woods?" The girl shot all these questions together, concerned seeing Doris in that peculiar condition.

"What? What do you really mean? Who are you to comment on my beach dress? This is the new, most expensive set I purchased recently. Look at yourself! *You* are wearing an old-fashioned, filthy gown and are commenting on my clothes? Do you even know who I am?" Doris rebuked.

The girl thought Doris was some poor girl who might have lost her mind and that was probably why she was roaming around like that. She felt a little pity yet tried to handle her in a polite manner.

"Oh, I beg your pardon, miss. I really did not have such intentions. You are taking me all wrong. I was not commenting on your clothes. It seems that you are not from this kingdom. However, these types of clothes are not welcome here. People would mind, should they see you in such an outfit—or 'without clothes' would be more appropriate. Perhaps, this must be common in your kingdom. Hmm … you may borrow my clothes … if needed." The young girl completed her sentence without taking a breath, shocked at having seen someone like.

"Woah, woah, woah! Wait! Give it a pause, Lady. What kingdom? What the hell are you talking about? You will give me clothes? Do I look like a tramp to you? I asked you a single question, and instead of answering me that, you are telling me God knows what! I think that I made a mistake asking you a question. Thanks, but no thanks! I'll look for the answers by myself." Saying that, Doris left her and moved toward the thick forest without listening to the girl in the hope that she would find someone else to answer her better.

She wandered all around for quite some time but could neither find anybody nor any end to this ordeal. She reached the same place where she had started. However, the only difference was that it was darker and colder now.

"Oh God! Not again. I reached here again! It seems that I am dead and in some kind of hell. Where should I go? What do I do? My clothes are all wet, and I just can't wear them. It's getting colder," she cried, feeling tired and looking up at the sky with fog.

Where is Doris?

Some twinkling stars were still visible. There was wonderful scenery around, but she was blind to the beauty, considering the situation she was in. She started shivering and was still reluctant to seek help from the girl she had had an argument with before. Apologizing was against her ego and pride. Therefore, she took out a towel from her bag and tried to cover herself as much as she could and sat against a large rock next to the brook in front of the girl's cottage and curled up into a tight ball to shield herself from the cold to whatever extent she could.

However, it was a forest, and she was sitting beside a brook. The cold rock was not helping either, but she had to be away from the dense bushes, as she was afraid of wild creatures. The cold started to take its toll on her. Tears started to flow from her eyes, and her nose started to run. She turned all pink and blue and started coughing and sneezing loudly.

The echo of her coughs and sneezes in the late, quiet evening made the girl come out. She saw and recognized Doris in no time. She went to her and noticed that Doris was in a terrible condition. Hence, she called her into her cottage. Doris tried to hold her for a little support, but the girl just stepped back and asked her to hold her shoulder, not her hands. Neither did Doris say anything, nor did she waste any time thinking considering her current situation. She just silently followed her, stumbling and shivering in the cold. The girl gave her warm clothes to wear and a blanket and made a fire to keep her guest warm. She tucket Doris in a blanket and fed her some hot supper in her bed as she still shivered and looked starved. Doris then covered herself till the head in the warmth of the blanket and blacked out almost immediately.

At Doris's house, her mother and father started to get worried about her. They waited long enough and decided to file a report to the police. Kate and Cyril were still there and were afraid, as they were the only ones to witness her last and had too absurd a story to make anybody believe them. The staff from the beach also did not witness that incident but they did not see Doris leave that place either.

Chapter 3

The New Place

The next morning, Doris yawned on the bed and said, "Oh, Rosie, tell mom that I'm not going to school today. My whole body aches. Will you get me a cup of coffee please?". Rosie was her maid.

She opened her eyes lazily and got up, startled. It was not her room. All the events of the earlier day flashed in her memory in an instant. Her eyes filled with tears as she realized that it was not some dream and was happening for real, that she was in a strange place without any explanation or a clue of how she ended up there. She took some time, wiped her eyes, and came out of the room looking for the girl.

"Ah, so you are awake. A very good morning. You were sick and out of all senses last night. How are you feeling now?" the girl asked, drying her clothes on a rope that was tied outside across two wood logs standing on the ground apart.

"I want to use your bathroom. Where may I go?" Doris asked without answering the girl's queries.

"Hm, there are so many bushes you can go to … anywhere," she replied innocently.

"What? Are you crazy?" Doris did not think that the girl was serious.

"No. Why would you say that? Oh, if you wish, you may use the chamber pot there. However, I use it only at night because of the darkness outside. During the day, since the pot is to be cleaned next to the brook anyway, I directly go over there," the girl tried to explain.

"Ew, gross! Don't tell me that you actually mean that? That 'go to the shrub' part or that bit about the chamber pot! We aren't stuck on some island, are we? Because that is the only thing that is making sense right now," Doris asked worried and was in fact disgusted by the thought of it.

"Of course not, miss. What makes you think we are stuck on an island? Although I wonder if you belong to a noble family … I have heard that they use garderobes." The other girl tried to understand what Doris was exactly asking for.

"Garderobes! Wha … what are you talking about?" Doris was confused.

"Privies?" The girl guessed all the options she knew so Doris could understand her. However, Doris remained unable to process the situation. "I do not understand whatever you are trying to say. Where do you exactly go for it then?" The girl was out of options and genuinely wanted to know what else Doris was looking for.

Doris could not really believe that the girl was unaware of such a basic thing. She was all confused about the place and her lifestyle. There was no sign of electricity or water supply and so on. She noticed the girl was taking water from the brook for her household chores.

She wondered whether it was some kind of island that the girl may have been stuck in for years or a city where people may have thrown her out as a result of some sin or crime she may have committed. However, nobody does that these days. There are jails for that. "Definitely stuck on an island," she said to herself without answering the girl.

Moreover, since the girl had done quite a favor to her by letting her spend the night at her home in such cruel weather last night, she thought about simply listening to her, although it was hard for Doris to follow her. She was out of other options anyway.

"I'm going there. All right, I'm going there," Doris said to her. Then, murmuring "Stupid girl. This is definitely some kind of joke or am I really in some kind of hell? Anyway, I have been to summer camps in my childhood, this is definitely worse than that, but I guess I can try just like I did those days and survived." to herself, she followed the brook upstream and went to a shrub to relieve herself.

While returning, her foot slipped on the marshy land, and she fell. The girl started laughing at her.

Doris got all dirty in the mud, and seeing the girl laughing at her, she lost the little patience she had. "What is so funny about this?" Doris asked, all annoyed.

"I must apologize. I didn't mean to laugh." The girl stopped laughing and extended the cloth she was holding to help Doris stand up.

"Ah … I have become so dirty. I must take a shower," Doris complained, ignoring the girl's help and dusting herself.

"You may go there." The girl pointed at her bathroom. It was a small area covered with some dirty old cloth with a wooden tub inside. "I'll give you water from the brook."

"That place? Do you call that a bathroom? Which poverty-stricken area do you live in? There is no toilet, no bathroom! Now, don't say that there is no shower, no tap, and no hot water?" Doris asked, surprised.

"Hot water? I can boil the water for you," the girl offered.

"You will have to boil water? Don't you have water heaters or geysers?" Doris was surprised. However, she immediately realized that her question wouldn't make any sense, considering the toilet.

"Hmm … geyser? What is that?" the girl asked, all confused.

"*Aargh!* I … I am really in hell! This water is so *cold*. Am I supposed to bathe in *this* water? Do you want me to *freeze to death*?" Doris said, touching the cold water.

"Stewhouses?" The girl tried to check if that was what Doris knew of at least, so they could come to a point. However, Doris said nothing but sighed heavily with disappointment.

"What is wrong?" the girl wanted to help.

"Don't you see? Everything is wrong. Do you bathe in this water?" Doris asked, shivering and shaking her hands to release some mud that was stuck.

"Yes, I bathe in that water. However, not very often. Fresh water is quite warm by itself. I can boil some water if that is cold for you," the girl offered again.

"Yes, please," Doris replied, rolling her eyes.

Then, she observed that her clothes were still wet. "Hey, my clothes are wet, so …" Doris again hesitated to ask for the girl's clothes.

"Oh, yes. Of course, you can take mine. I am glad to help." Saying that, the girl gave a pair of her clothes to Doris, who then bathed and came out, shivering.

"I am going to the market to sell these pies and muffins. I have kept some breakfast for you in the kitchen. I am running late. You can stay here as long as you want to. You are my guest, and I should be happy to have some company here. Spend the day as you please in here." The girl smiled graciously.

"Hey, hold on! Market? You mean there are more people around? And this is not an island you're stuck in alone?" Doris asked, all amazed.

"Certainly not. This is not an island. Why do you keep asking this? And yes, there are so many people around here," the girl replied.

Doris assumed that girl was crazy to be living out there alone and in such a way. Thinking as much, she said, "I think you have the impression that I am a beggar or some poor person who needs your mercy. But for your kind information, I am not any of them. I have money, and I can buy anything I want from the market. So, thanks for your help so far and for offering me breakfast."

Then, she took out some money from her bag.

"So, tell me how much I owe you," she asked, showing her the money she had.

"What? How much can helping someone in such a lost condition cost? If you can count, then count and give me. I will happily take it." The girl felt insulted now.

"Ah … so, you want me to give you all my money? Here, take it. I knew it. I mean I was wondering too how a person could be so generous! And you finally show me your true intentions. Take it," Doris said, giving her the money.

"I do not have such intentions at all, first of all. I do not need anything from you. However, what kind of thing is this?" the girl asked Doris very innocently again, observing the notes in her hand.

"So, now, you don't even know what this thing is? Do you think I am a fool, or are you so poor that you have never seen these notes with your eyes? Or do you use some other currency around here?"

"Notes?" the girl asked, all confused.

"Ugh! You are driving me nuts now. Are you kidding me? I mean, what do you get after selling these muffins then?" Doris asked, frustrated at the girl's lack of awareness and stupidity.

"Copper or silver. Some people exchange them for other products. Rich people give me gold when I cook for their big functions or celebrations." But the girl again replied in all innocence and wondered what else she might get.

"What? Are you serious?" Doris was surprised again.

"Yes. What else do people get after selling things in your kingdom?"

"Hm … these notes," Doris said, looking at the notes, all confused on her own.

"It's all right. These things you're calling 'notes' or whatever have no value here. Moreover, they will not help you buy anything here. Keep them to yourself. I forgive you for whatever you just said," the girl replied, as she felt bad that Doris offered her money for her help.

"But I thought that US dollars were valued everywhere," she said, scratching her head and feeling all confused.

"I'm afraid I do not know what … US … notes you're talking about. They do not work here in our kingdom," the girl said.

"Kingdom? Is this Europe?" Doris genuinely queried, catching onto the word "kingdom" the girl kept repeating for everything.

"Europe?" The girl did not understand this as well.

"Is this some kind of prank show?" Doris paused a little, thinking about this possibility.

"What?" The girl didn't know the meaning of that either.

"Yeah, I know. It is a big *prank* show I am in! I mean, what else could it be? Come on, you had me fooled so far. Good one!" Doris now believed that she knew what was happening for a while. "Oh, come out now. It was hilarious. Haha. But I got you now. Come out, you all!" Doris screamed, looking around.

However, the girl just stood there, trying to understand how mental Doris could be.

"Where are the cameras?" Doris now asked the girl.

"Look, we clearly do not speak each other's language, although it seems to be the same. And I am afraid to say this, but I think that you are losing your mind—maybe due to the cold last night. It *was* too bad. Take some rest until you recollect where you come from. It is all fine with me. I am getting late, so please excuse me," the girl said.

Doris said nothing. She definitely had no words to say.

"And goodbye. Hope you come to your senses soon," the girl wished her and left.

There definitely was something that Doris was unaware of too—some lack of understanding—maybe because of that diary she was pulled into, and Doris understood this at least after the girl left.

Doris watched the girl and compared herself with her. She herself was bad and ill tempered, whereas the girl was only extremely helpful and tolerated her so generously! She was feeling awkward and shameful about her own behavior, and so, she left the place too, as she was too embarrassed to stay back there and ask the girl anymore favors. She positively thought that she would find someone else now. However, as she was unaware of the place and was lost in that forest the day before, she thought about quietly following the girl without letting her know so she could find more people. Nevertheless, since the girl was moving so fast, Doris lost her way again and moved in a different direction.

The Guy

She entered the dense forest to look for a city or at least a person who could tell her where she exactly was, on her own. She was thinking about that girl and moving forward.

However, she was now feeling hungry and thirsty after reaching the thick forest. She suddenly recalled that she had her cellphone.

"Oh, there is no bigger fool than me. Haha! I have my phone with me, and I'm roaming here like an idiot," she said with happiness, searching for it in her bag. She found it, but perhaps, her fate was not with her at that time. The phone was dead. The power bank suddenly was dead too. "Strange, at least my power bank was fully charged." She tried but failed to get any kind of connectivity.

"Oh, come on. Please … please … is this some kind of revenge for something? Damn it. This stupid phone had to be dead at this time. Crap! What will I do now? That girl offered me breakfast, but I … had to save my ego. Those muffins smelled amazing, but I rejected them. There is no bigger fool than me in this whole world. Now, if I go back there to her for help, she will get me arrested. Oh, I'm so horrible." She now regretted her own behavior.

"I am in such a thick bloody forest with no coffee, no snacks, no mom or dad, and in such a condition, my cellphone is not working as well. I think God is punishing me for something. This is even crueler than being grounded!" Doris complained to herself.

There were carpets of ferns all around and a beautiful forest, and daffodils were moving in the direction of the wind through the ferns. The fragrance of different flowers filled the air with the chirrup of birds. Huge trees and small wild creatures were also in her surroundings. Beautiful nature and a refreshing breeze were all around her. It was like paradise. But she was not enjoying the beauty around her. That heaven was almost hell for her.

She walked for quite some time but did not reach any end. However, luckily, in that starvation, she found an apple tree right in front of her.

"Oh, good God! Oh God! Hope it's not a mirage … an apple tree! Thank God! Nice fresh breakfast. But … but … doesn't it seem surprisingly high? Apples don't grow that high. Moreover, it looks like someone has plucked all the apples within human reach. Good lord, there is no one to pluck them for me. What do I do now? Let's give it a try at least. There's nobody around to witness me do this anyway." She was talking to herself in her solitude.

She tried climbing the tree a few times but failed.

"Oh, first, I am lost. Second, I am hungry. Third, I have a huge apple tree in front of my eyes, but I can't climb it, and fourth, I am wearing this heavy and long stupid gown that is just adding right to the happiest moment of my life." She was frustrated and, murmuring with sarcasm, tried climbing the tree once again. Suddenly, she slipped and fell.

Doris heard the loud voice of a man laughing. Seated where she had fallen, she turned and saw a young man laughing at her. But when his eyes met Doris's, he stopped laughing as she stared at him in embarrassment and because he found himself falling for her personal charm and childish behavior. He had never seen such a beauty before. Doris was staring at him, but he could feel a tickling sensation in his body. She was a perfect treat for his eyes as well as his heart. Her messy hair and her beautiful hands fixing them … he was observing it all. He was silent suddenly.

Doris, although a little happy to finally see a person, broke the silence in both agitation and embarrassment. "What? What is it with you all here finding people falling so amusing?"

"Hmm … my sincerest apologies, miss," he said politely, offering her his hand to help her stand.

"Apologies? Do you even know who I am? How dare you laugh at me?" Doris started snubbing him and stood up on her own.

He didn't say anything. He just looked at her clothes and smiled slightly.

"Hey, don't you judge me based on my clothes, all right? I am lost. A girl gave me her clothes to wear because mine were wet.

I know these are horrible and funny looking, but you don't have any right to judge me," she explained.

"Ah, I see! I did not mean to offend you at all, miss," he said politely.

Doris, for the first time, took note of the man's appearance. He was dressed like a medieval knight and carrying a sword on his waist. She couldn't help but notice there was a shiny dark brown horse not very far, grazing and carrying the man's possessions. The man was magnificent enough to be swooned over.

"Hey, is this real? Why are you carrying it? I am seeing someone carry a sword for the first time in my life. I've probably seen them only in some theme hotels or in front of some European castles. Is there some kind of theme party in your city for which you are all dressed like this? And what's with the horse? Man, you are embodying your character—whatever that is—very well" she asked curiously. Doris was barely in the condition to question him as she was wearing a borrowed, tatty dress herself. But still, she wasn't noticing herself at that time and thought that only a silly man would stroll in the middle of a forest with a sword and a horse.

"Yes, of course, it is real. Why do you ask that? And that is my stallion, Maddox. He is my pal," the man replied walking towards him.

"Maddox! Good name. My dad owns a horse too. His name is Needles. He is one of the best! Bet he would defeat Maddox in a race." Doris suddenly took interest in the conversation since she struck something common, walking along with him.

The man laughed. "Well, I think you underestimate Maddox. He is the best here as well," the man said, rubbing Maddox's mane as he had reached him by then.

"Oh, I doubt that. Needles wins all races. He is invincible." Doris lit up talking about her horse.

"Well, that is a strong statement. Maddox is the fastest one I know too," the man replied, smiling. "Aren't you, my friend?" he continued, patting Maddox.

"No offense to you, boy, but we will see that when my Needles beats you to dust." Doris was proud of her horse too.

"We shall indeed see that." The man accepted the challenge.

"By the way, I have been observing you for a while. Why were you climbing this tree?" He was curious to know what Doris was doing.

"You were watching me climb the tree and … and yet you continued just watching without helping me, only to mock me later?" she asked.

"But why were you climbing the tree?" he asked again.

"Because I like climbing trees. I am hungry, you dumb man!" she answered sarcastically.

"Excuse me," he said.

Bratty as she was, she did not say anything further and tried to climb the tree again, hoping that he would help her on his own—which is what women expect: a man to understand them in such situations and help them without letting them ask for it. But poor men, they never understand. And so was the case with this person.

"It seems that you do not belong to this place." He was surprised to see this behavior in a girl. He just stood and watched Doris struggle. Not that he wasn't a gentleman or so, he was just trying to understand why she wasn't asking him for help instead.

"Oh, yeah! Good observation. I don't belong to this place. I am lost. Lost in this God-forsaken place," she told him while struggling to climb.

"Yes, that makes perfect sense. I knew it because I have never seen you here before," he said, wondering.

"Hmm ... but what are you doing here in this forest? Spying on lost people, eh? Or only girls?" she asked, and with that, she fell again.

He smiled at her clumsiness too. "Excuse me, my dear. May I?" he asked, offering her his hand again.

"Sure," she said, holding his hand to stand this time.

He climbed the tree high, taking Maddox's help, and plucked some apples for her. The moment he offered the apples to Doris, she grabbed them and gobbled them like a savage.

The young, charming man stared at her eating like that and just smiled.

"Er ... all right, all right, please slow down. They are not running away anywhere," the young man interrupted.

"Hmm ... I know ... Thanks, by the way," Doris said with her mouth full.

"My pleasure, miss." He bowed respectfully.

"Oh ... by the way, do you happen to have a cellphone on you by any chance?" she asked him while still eating.

The man reacted as if he had heard the word "cellphone" for the first time. "And what is that? Cell ... pho-phone?" he asked.

"What? Do you really not know what a phone is?" she asked, surprised. She was hoping that the next person she found would be normal at least. But it turned out she had no luck. "You all must be kidding, right?"

"No, I really could not catch what you just said," he replied.

"Then, I really can't explain it."

"It's all right if you cannot explain. Nonetheless, I must tell you that your hair looks amazing! It looks so ... different," he said, staring at them.

"I know. My stylist is the best," she said, unconsciously blushing. "But now, don't tell me that you don't know what a stylist means," she continued, realizing he might say he had not heard her words.

"Yes, you are correct about that. Your maid, perhaps?" he asked innocently.

"A ... uh-huh. Oh God, it's really annoying now," she cried.

"What happened, miss? What is bothering you so much?" He wanted to know.

"Nothing. Just do me a favor, will you?"

"Yes, I shall be glad to."

"Could you please tell me where I can find someone sane?" she asked bluntly.

"Pardon me, I ... I am a sane person. Why do you have doubts about that? What do you want to know? Ask me away, and I shall try to answer you," he replied, a bit embarrassed.

"Oh, please," she said and started moving away from him.

"Hey! Where are you going?" he asked.

"Where am I going? I am trying to find someone ... someone who can tell me where on earth I am," she said, frustrated.

"I can tell you that. You are in Gwynedd. In the kingdom of King Dafydd ap Llywelyn," he answered.

"What? Never heard of such a strange name," Doris said while still walking, but her speed reduced as she processed that man's statement. However, since it didn't make any sense to her, she started to walk faster again. But the young man didn't want her to leave.

"Hey, why are you going away? It was not some joke." He tried to stop her.

"I know. I didn't laugh. I was just being sarcastic. You understand that at least?"

The man was all blank.

"You know what? If only I could say, 'You must be kidding me. Goodbye!'" She tried to get rid of him because even though he was so unimaginably handsome, he was just annoying her by not knowing anything again, just like the last girl she met, and this was only freaking her out.

"Hey! Wait. You did not tell me your name yet. And where do you live? Do you not think we should meet again?" he asked hesitatingly.

"What would you do with my name? I don't tell strangers my name. And there is no way we will meet again. I mean I might have found you interesting if I found you under normal circumstances. But like this, I don't want to go crazy. And I don't belong to this place anyway … in your words, this kingdom." She started to move faster.

"Then, which place are you from?" he asked.

"Florida. Have you ever heard this name in your life?" she asked him annoyed, knowing by now that he most certainly didn't know the place.

"Hmmm … no. However, tell me about this place properly," he asked politely.

"Villa 15, Summer Bay Plaza, Deen Still Road, Clermont, Florida, USA. There you go. I bet you didn't get a word of what I just said, did you?" Doris stopped and answered him, knowing that he wouldn't catch any of it.

"Aye … there is no such road or place called Deen Still or Florida of all the places I know. We have a royal deer park though," he muttered.

"What?" she asked.

"Oh, nothing. I meant I can help you find your home," he said very graciously.

"No, please. Can't you just leave me alone? I feel like crying now," she cried.

"But I can help you."

"I don't need your help. Thanks for the apples, and goodbye." Saying that, she moved swiftly out of the place.

Chapter 5

An Attack

She moved ahead and found no end to the thick forest. It was a long and difficult path. She could see a lot of squirrels, badgers running around, some deer grazing at distance and so many types of different birds that she had never seen before, which somehow mesmerized her. However, she could not gather any courage to approach any of them. It was more like a wildlife safari for her without any guide. She was having mixed feelings, a little bit of excitement finding such adorable creatures, a bit of disgust and fear on seeing snakes, insects or spiders out there in the open, a little bit of hope to find an end to that place, fatigue, as she had been walking for a long time, frustrated on not knowing where she was. Moreover, she also could not help but think about the boy she had met before.

Was that man completely crazy? How could he be so stupid? He seemed to be from a good background and was dreamy beyond any limits, but along with these qualities, he also seemed to be a complete idiot. Are these people playing with me? Is this some place for madmen? Oh, yes! That seems to be the case. This whole place is filled with

An Attack

crazy people who are wandering free. And I am stuck here among these people! That girl was talking crap too, and that man has never heard of Florida or the USA! And … why was he carrying a sword? They were definitely crazy. Doris was lost in her own thoughts and did not know what a thick forest could bring forth. She was only walking ahead. However, a forest is never a safe place, especially for an unarmed person …

She heard and saw something moving in the shrubs in front of her. She put one step forward curiously toward it when a huge bear, snorting, came out and lurched toward her. She screamed in terror and closed her eyes with her arms, as it was too close. Running could not have helped her anyway. She could not do anything except stand there and accept her fate. All of a sudden, with the roar of the bear, she also heard the sound of a horse's hooves. When she opened her eyes, she found Maddox rearing in front of the bear and neighing with the same young man riding him. She was shaking and sweating with fear.

"Go away! I shall handle it. You please just run," he shouted while taking guard against the beast when Maddox hit the bear with his hooves and bought some time for the man to get down.

"What are you doing here?" she shouted, trembling.

"Do not question me at this moment! Just go away …" he requested, pulling his sword out.

Suddenly, the bear swung its paws and scratched his arm.

"Ouch!" Doris yelped as he did too.

The bear now started to attack him, while Doris kept on screaming without moving from her place. Her mind, in fact, had blanked out. The boy understood the situation and knew he couldn't fight the beast any longer, so he drew his sword and stabbed it so hard in its neck that it died instantly and fell on him.

"You killed it ... You killed it! Oh my God! You just killed a bear," she cried, watching it die in front of her.

"Will you please help me out here?" he asked, being stuck under it and extending his hand for help.

"Was it really necessary to kill it?" She was furious as she had never seen such violence in her life before.

"So, what did you expect? Let that bear kill one of us? I would be really happy if you thank me instead or at least help me get out of this now." He was still lying under the lifeless bear.

"Oh ... I am sorry. Are you alright?" She helped him come out.

The moment he stood, she hit him hard on his arm. "Why did you kill it?" asked Doris again.

But since she hit him where he was hurt, he couldn't help but scream in pain, holding his arm.

She saw that the shirt on his arm was torn. He had a scratch there, and it was bleeding. He had a few bruises too and seemed to be in pain. His ivory shirt was quite red with blood. A bit of his own and a bit of the bear's. She searched for something in her bag and took out a cloth. She then gently tied the cloth around his arm. He was happy looking at her anxious and caring for him. To gain some more sympathy, he screamed. But Doris took no time to understand that he was pretending now.

"Oh, stop overacting now," she said, blushing.

"Hmm …" He grinned.

"You should get a tetanus injection or whatever else it is they give you here after being scratched or bitten by a wild animal like this bear," Doris suggested, a bit concerned.

"Tetanus?" He didn't get what Doris meant.

"Oh … This is a nightmare! Anyway, who the hell asked you to fight it? Why were you trying to be a hero? We could have just run away," she asked, helping him stand.

"Did it really look that easy to you? I did not want to kill it either. I asked you to run so I could run too. But you did not, and I did not see any other way, so I killed it as the situation demanded," he explained.

"Woah! Woah! Hold on. Are you blaming me?" Doris asked.

"No, I mean had you run when I asked you to, I might not have killed it." He tried to explain without getting into an argument.

"So, that's my fault? And by the way, how did you reach here in no time to save me? Were you following me?" Doris was not quitting the fight.

"Er …" He had nothing to answer because he really had been following her.

"Oh, you were, weren't you?" She understood.

"But ... but I saved you, you were in this forest all alone." he said, all confused.

"Oh, so, that is how you win an argument?" she asked.

"But I am not arguing." He didn't know how to talk to her anymore.

"Okay, well, thank you so much for your help. And I hope not to see you ever again." She started to move again.

"Wait ... stay." Despite all this, he didn't want her to go.

She stopped and asked, "Why should I?"

"Because I did not mean to pick a fight with you in case we just fought. Also, I can see that you are in some trouble, and that perfectly explains why you feel so annoyed and frustrated. And it would be my pleasure to help you in any way." The gentleman tried his best to calm Doris and really start over on good terms.

Well, these words impressed Doris to her heart. It was the first time she felt someone really understood her. She now looked at him again and realized how charming he was and couldn't say anything. But she just turned back and started to walk, as she knew he wouldn't be able to help her.

The man simply stood there and saw her walk away. He couldn't do or say anything more to make her stop. Disappointed, he walked back with Maddox.

After some time, she realized that she was too rude to him. After all, he had saved her life from that beast. If it hadn't been for him arriving on time, she would not even be alive. Also, after all this, instead of taking care of him and escorting him home in his

An Attack

injured condition, she abandoned him in the middle of a forest. These thoughts made her feel remorseful. So, she retraced her steps but found no one there.

"Oh, what have I done? He saved my life after all, and I ... I fought with him! What is wrong with me? Why can't I talk to people nicely?" She was nothing but sorry ... again. Too much was going on around her. It was a big change for her to process. She felt exhausted and didn't know what to do or whom to trust at that point. However, she didn't want to be this mean to someone. She couldn't help but sob in her solitude. "I miss home," she said with tears in her eyes.

There, Kate and Cyril had been questioned and bothered about Doris at the police station. They were not arrested, as their parents had come to their rescue too with their lawyers. They returned to their homes. Kate had the book with her, and she was disturbed and afraid too, wondering what could have really happened to Doris. Nobody believed them. She just looked at the book and wondered how something like that could have happened. When she opened the book again, she found a few of its pages had something written on them. She was surprised to see this, as she clearly recalled that they were completely blank when they first saw the book as well as when she last saw it while showing it to the police. She called Cyril and started to read it. It documented some of the events that had been happening to Doris after she was lost.

"Why did she not take any help from him?" Cyril yelled.

Kate was happy that they had some proof to present to Doris's parents. She ran to them with the book. Doris's parents were shocked to see that, but they thought maybe it was what Kate had written just to prove their story. Kate and Cyril themselves found what had happened hard to believe, even though they saw it all happen in front of their eyes—let alone Doris's parents, who didn't even witness everything.

Kate and Cyril were very disappointed and left for their places again.

"What do we do now, Kate?" Cyril asked.

"I don't know," Kate answered with a long face. "Where are you, Doris?" She started crying.

"Hey … she will be fine. Don't you know? She is Doris. We must rather be worried about the people she's going to meet or be with." Cyril tried to console her.

Kate smiled with tears of worry still in her eyes.

"Hey, don't you do that to me. At least, we can know what is happening to her. I don't care what people think. We just know what happened, as insane as it sounds. We know that she is fine. At least until now. And we have each other to believe, especially in this case," Cyril said to Kate.

"Oh, Cyril, I just love you." She hugged him.

"What?" Cyril was surprised.

Kate didn't say anything and hugged him tighter.

Doris's parents were extremely worried about her now. They started to think of the possibility that Kate and Cyril might have killed her or something. Hundreds of thoughts start to appear when a child goes missing. Being clueless about where she could be started bringing the worst nightmares to Doris's parents, which put them in a terrible condition.

Chapter 6

Back to Her

It was dawn again. The birds were chirping and flying to their nests. The small animals in the jungle were also moving toward their respective homes. Doris was watching all of them with wet eyes. She thought that even those animals had their homes to return to that day, but she did not. She was helpless, homeless, tired, and hungry, just gabbing at those lucky animals.

"Oh, you are still here?" Doris heard a familiar voice from behind.

Doris turned around to find the same girl she surprisingly met again and again, but this time, Doris just jumped and hugged her. "Oh, you are here!"

The girl was first confused but then smiled and embraced Doris, a little conscious about her hands not touching her.

"Wait, was I wandering again in circles? How am I ever gonna find my way back home this way?" Doris said with the long face, realizing this.

Maybe her fate brought her back to that girl over and over again. Maybe someone wanted her to just meet that girl and get to know her.

"This means you have not found your way back home yet?" the girl asked.

"No ... No, I have not," Doris answered helplessly.

"Oh, I'm so sorry. Where are you planning to stay for the night?" she asked politely.

"I don't ... I don't know," Doris said, hesitating.

"Why do you not come to my place?" the girl invited her with a smile.

"Are you really inviting me to your house? After everything I said to you earlier?" Doris asked, surprised and shy now.

"Yes, of course! Why should I not?" the girl replied.

"But ... but until when will you help me?" Doris asked.

"Until you find your way back home," the girl replied with the most beautiful and generous smile.

Her words made Doris so overwhelmed that she immediately hugged her tightly again. "I am so sorry for behaving so badly." She felt guilty about her behavior. She realized that those she called crazy and insulted so much repeatedly were the ones who helped her in that completely strange place. "Thank you so much! Thanks a lot. And I'm so sorry about my behavior." Doris had no other words left to say to her.

"Oh, it is completely all right. I am glad to help you. You are in trouble. I can see that. Let us go," the girl said. "By the way, you never told me your name. What is your name?" she added to make her feel acquainted.

"My name is Doris. Doris Wilson. And what's yours?" Doris asked.

"Christine," the girl replied.

They reached the cottage, talking.

"So, you live here alone? In this quiet and terrible place?" Doris asked.

"Well, yes," Christine replied while keeping her stuffs on a table and losing some of her heavy clothes.

"But why? Why do you live like this?" Doris asked.

"I am sorry, but I don't follow what you are exactly trying to ask. Everyone lives like this unless they are noble or royal. The only difference is I live here alone." Christine could not understand what manner of living standard Doris was expecting a common person to have.

"Noble and royal? Is this Europe? But how am I in Europe? Girl, you really sound very strange. Anyway, what I was trying to ask you is why you live alone. Away from others, in the middle of such a dense forest? Doesn't it seem horrible to you?" Doris asked.

"Haha! It is perhaps a horrible place for you because you are lost here, but this place is perfect for me. I love my solitude. Away from the miseries and the hard times the nobles give to others. Here, they mostly don't dare to come. Or they don't even know that I exist. Besides, I can feel the fresh air in the morning, the chirping of birds, the sounds of small, lovely creatures—"

"And the roar of wild bears," Doris interrupted with her sarcasm.

Christine laughed at Doris's words. "You are funny." Christine walked into her kitchen to prepare something for dinner.

"I mean, really, haven't you ever encountered any wild animals here?" Doris was curious about her lonely life. She was following Christine to clear her doubts.

"Haha! No. Fortunately, I have never come across any ferocious animals here yet. Maybe I have been lucky so far," Christine replied, laughing.

"This means only my luck is rotten," Doris said.

"Haha! I said that casually, but it has nothing to do with luck. Everything happens for a reason. But why were you asking?" Christine asked.

"Because a bear attacked me today," Doris told her.

"A bear? Are you all right, my dear? How did you manage to save yourself from that?" Christine asked.

"I was so terrified, and I thought it was the end of my life. I just closed my eyes, but a young man helped me … He fought that bear for me." Doris told her about everything that had happened.

"See, I told you everything happens for a reason," Christine said, nudging Doris to lighten her mood.

"Haha, why would you say that?" Doris blushed.

"Hm … maybe because you had to meet that young man. Come on, tell me about him. Was he handsome?" Christine teased Doris.

"Oh … forget it." Doris shied away.

"No, seriously. Was he handsome? What was his name? Maybe I can help you meet him again," Christine continued.

"Now, you're going too far. Please leave this topic. I was asking about you. Why do you live here alone?" Doris asked.

"Hm … I was only an infant when my parents threw me here near this brook. An old woman who used to live here heard me crying in the cold, took me, and raised me as her own. See, she helped a little helpless child in the same way I helped you. It is what I have learned from her after all. Had she not taken me, I might not be here alive," Christine answered with a sad smile, talking about her foster mother.

"So, where is that woman now?" Doris asked, looking around.

"She is no more. She also left me alone two years ago. I did not know she was not my real mother until she took her last breath. When she realized that she would not live anymore, she decided to tell me the truth. I do not even know who my real parents are, and you know what? I do not even want to know who those people are who gave birth to me and threw me here. I surely would have died, but that lady gave me a new life. That is why I call her my mother. She is my mother, and nobody else is. And now, I am an orphan because my mother is not here with me," Christine said with grief.

"Oh, I'm so sorry. Please don't cry," Doris said.

"No, my apologies. I did not mean to. I think I got carried away. Well, tell me something else. Tell me something about you," Christine asked, changing the topic.

Doris told her exactly what had happened with her and how she reached there and got lost. Christine was not exactly getting what Doris was trying to tell her, but the only thing that she understood was that something magical had happened with Doris.

Doris asked her about the name of the place.

"This is the kingdom of Gwynedd. Sorry to say this, but I did not get most of what you told me. Your whereabouts, the high school, skipping classes, and plenty of other things! Women allowed to be educated! What is this world you are talking about! I really did not catch you. The only thing I understand is that you are lost and in trouble. And I shall help you find your way back home. I shall take you with me to the market of our kingdom so that you can find a way," Christine comforted Doris.

"A ... Wait, about this kingdom. This sounds very strange. Am I in a European country? Because there are none in America, as far as I know. And trust me, I have been in Europe several times, but Gwynedd? I wish my geography was good enough to recognize this place, or at least, I wish my phone worked so I could Google it right away." Doris was trying to find out about the place.

"Amer-ee-ca?" Christine could not understand what Doris was talking about again.

"Okay. So, your geography is worse than mine. And it must be really bad if you do not know where America is. Have you never been to school? What era are you living in?" Doris wondered how she was unaware of the US.

"Schools! Only higher-class men are privileged enough for that," Christine answered.

"Anyway, I know a little about the monarchy in Europe if this place is on that continent. I know about Queen Elizabeth II—now, King Charles is the monarch—and a little about monarchies still existing in Bhutan and Japan and a few other countries. But I have never heard of this name, Gwynedd!"

"A-and you say you do not understand me! What are you saying? This is really a very complicated conversation! And who is Queen Elizabeth?" Christine asked, confused.

"Don't you really know her?" Doris was more surprised now.

"You don't know what a phone is, USA, Queen Elizabeth. What a sad life you must be living because you stay here alone in the woods. I understand you were raised by an old woman in the woods, and you must have started liking staying here alone. But this is why you should not cut contact with the outside world so much that you do not even know what a phone is!" Doris believed that staying isolated with an old woman and maybe in poverty was the reason for Christine's lack of awareness of the things Doris was referring to.

"I have not cut myself out from the world. I meet so many people every day. Besides, I spend almost my entire day in our market. I get to know about things that are prominent in our kingdom at least. I am very certain that nobody I know is aware of the word 'fone'. And what is this thing you are speaking of continuously? How does it look? Maybe we call this thing by some other name here." Christine was still without a clue about what Doris was referring to.

Doris took out her phone from her bag and showed it to the girl to kill the confusion. "This thing!"

"Is it something within this flat box?" Christine thought it was some box.

"No, it's not a box! *This* is a phone." Doris didn't know how to react at this point.

"What does one do with this thing?" Christine said, trying to touch it, and was sure now that she had never seen a phone before.

"Don't you know? People who are far away talk to each other with this," Doris tried to explain again.

"Ah … no! Really? This must belong to sorcerers." Christine was thrilled to know about the existence of such a thing.

"Sorcerers? No. At least everybody I know has one," Doris said.

"What a wonderful thing this is then. I would love to see your kingdom. It sounds very interesting." Christine was curious.

"Are you sure you don't know anybody with this in your kingdom? Because if anyone has this, I can contact my parents. I am sure plenty of people ask about online payment since you have a bakery," Doris asked.

"I do not think so. On-line pay-men? Also, if you can really talk to a person who is far away as you claim, then why do you not talk to your parents with it? You have this." Christine had a genuine query.

"Yeah, you have a point there, but it comes with the problem of network range and battery. Now, I realize that you are probably not aware of battery and network too, are you?"

Christine just nodded in agreement.

"Huh … Forget it! This is getting irritating now. I do not have the energy to explain so many basic things right now." Doris was tired of making people understand the stuff they were unaware of.

She noticed that Christine wore gloves the whole time. So, she just asked her casually, "Why are you wearing that thing even at home by the way?"

"Hm, oh, I just like wearing it," Christine replied consciously.

"Take it off. It does not even look good or match your dress. So out of fashion, if you ask me." Doris gave her opinion.

"Er, this is not for fashion. It is actually because I work at a bakery. I need to keep my hands clean. Moreover, it was given to me by my mother, so I like to wear it all the time." Christine explained while continuing her chorus.

"That's so lame. You wear this all the time to keep your hands clean?" Doris asked. "That's really hygienic if you ask me though." Doris giggled.

"Also, it surely helps me with the extra cold that we have here in the forest." Christine was not ready to take off the gloves for some reason.

"Okay, whatever. Anyway, if you were in my place, I would have never spoken to you after hearing those freaky reasons to wear gloves all the time." Doris sighed, thinking it was none of her business.

She started to think about the man she had met in the woods. She took a while, and something struck her mind. "I do not understand one thing." Doris broke the silence.

"What?" Christine asked while serving dinner.

"I understand that since you are living alone, you are unaware of these basic things. But why was that man also unaware of everything I was saying? He seemed to have a good background. How did he not understand me either?" Doris tried to bring things to a conclusion.

"Still thinking about that man from the woods, eh? He must be a nobleman, I believe. Lucky you," Christine said, smiling.

"Oh, please, I am thinking of something else. It is hard to digest that not a single person in your kingdom is aware of a phone," Doris wondered while having her supper. But suddenly, one thing crossed her mind. "Hey, I know! I entered a book! Yes, I entered a book. This is true, and it could also be true that I am in the past ... in history! Was that book a time machine? But how could that be? How can a book be a machine? Not sure what the logic is behind it, but this surely seems to be some other era. Our beliefs and expectations seem to be generations apart," Doris said.

"Err … I am still not able to understand what you're trying to say!" Christine was now doubting Doris's sanity.

"But I understand everything now! That's why you and that man were talking about a kingdom. That's why you don't know what dollars and cellphones are. That's why you are wearing these old-fashioned clothes! No offense, by the way. That's why that man was carrying a sword and was with a horse—maybe he was hunting—and that's why he too has never heard of USA! And you both speak with such excessive politeness and show dated manners. I have hardly heard someone talk like this, except in some movies based in medieval times. I have been wondering if I was teleported someplace else, but that does not make as much sense as this does. Yes, this could happen … Oh yes, this is what is happening here!" Doris could understand some things that were happening to her. This may have been a nightmare, but her entering a book really did happen. So, why couldn't being transported to history be a possibility?

"Unbelievable! Impossible!" Christine too understood something now about what Doris was trying to say for the first time. But it was not possible for her to accept that she was in the past and a part of a book. She was living in her reality. And according to what Doris was trying to say, Christine was not even real or didn't exist anymore in Doris's reality.

"Yes! Nothing is impossible. Haven't you heard? Okay, come on, tell me which century this is according to you?"

"Hmm … the 13th century," Christine replied, confused.

"What? Unbelievable. So, it *is* true! See … I was right." She was a little happy that she had a clue about what was actually happening.

"By the way … Hi, I am Doris from the 21st century!" Doris continued introducing herself again and extending her hand for a shake.

"What! That just cannot be possible. You are playing with me, aren't you?" Christine gazed at Doris with astonishment.

"No, I am not. It's true. Don't you see? We do not know each other at all. I mean, century wise. Do you have any other explanation for this?"

Christine was silent and trying to get hold of what Doris was saying.

"But the problem is—how do I get out of this book, and when?" Doris asked, realizing the depth of her trouble now.

Christine was unable to believe all those things, but she could see there was no reason for Doris to lie. Also, as innocent as Christine was, she somehow believed her a bit. "So, you mean to say that you have come from the future!" This was by far the only exciting or out-of-the-ordinary thing that had happened to Christine in her entire life. "Then, what is different about the time you have come from?" Christine was curious.

"We do not have kingdoms so commonly, first of all," Doris replied.

"Then?" Christine wondered.

"We live in a democracy. People make their own government. There are monarchies too but not everywhere," Doris tried to explain.

"This demo-cr-crazy sounds interesting, but how would a country and its people be managed without a king?" Christine wanted to know something about the future.

"There is something called a 'government', which is selected by the citizens themselves. People can do whatever they want, except for crimes. No one rules over others. Or that is what we think," Doris replied.

"But why has this king system ended in your time?" Christine was curious.

"Because nobody can rule over anyone's life! And the kings started to think that they had the right to rule upon their people. Since nobody could challenge them or question them, they could rule over anyone's life. Woah, I feel so brilliant knowing so much more than you." Doris was thrilled to explain all these things to Christine.

"But our king is not at all like that. He is so kind and does so much for his people. He is absolutely generous," Christine disagreed.

"That is not the point. It is not just your king. I am not saying that your king is bad … but it doesn't mean that every king in the future will be nice like him. Maybe the next king will be a bad one!" Doris tried to explain.

"You mean the prince! Not at all! He is not even the slightest of bad. He is even nicer than our present king. He is kind, sweet, generous, and the handsomest person you will ever see. Every girl in the kingdom dies to even have a glance at him. Oh and …" Christine started admiring the prince so much with all excitement that it bewitched her all of a sudden.

"Oooh, look who is enchanted by the charms of a prince!" Doris immediately caught what Christine wanted to say and how her eyes sparkled while talking about the prince, and being a straightforward girl, she said this upfront, teasing her.

"No … I did not mean that. You must be joking." Christine tried to deny this but couldn't hide her blushing.

"Oh, come on. Are you trying to fool me? I am Doris. No one can fool me so easily, especially in matters like this. And I got what you wanted to say. I only gave you an example, and you just took it so personally. You started admiring him so much! Don't lie to me," Doris teased her.

"Ah … No, he is a prince, and I work in a bakery. No way. Besides, do not even speak of this to anyone. Otherwise, they shall either make fun of me or think wrong of me." Christine tried to refuse her claim.

"I am not asking who is who. I am just asking; do you like him or not? And why do you care about what anyone would think of you anyway?" Now, Doris asked her directly.

"I do not know. He is so handsome … and so nice. He is the only man I think about. Last time I saw him, I just felt my heart pounding so loud or maybe skipping a beat. I thought about him for months. I only wish that I could talk to him someday." Now, Christine finally accepted the truth.

"Oh, you're really crazy. See, I got you," Doris said with joy.

"Yes, you caught me. But I insist that you do not speak of this to anyone," Christine requested.

"All right. As if I know anyone else in town. But you know, I think he is not a kind person. He can't see so much love for him in a young pretty girl's eyes in his own kingdom." Doris simply put forth her thoughts.

"No, that is so not true. He is nice. Moreover, every girl is as crazy about him as I am. He has never seen me too. It is not his fault. Besides, he is the crown prince. He can never marry someone like me anyway. He can marry only a royal or a noble. And I am nobody. I am not even aware of my own background. Even if I were to say my foster mother was my own, I do not have any dowry to give. So, this is only a sweet dream. Otherwise, I could not even possibly imagine him looking at me that way," Christine explained.

"What? Dowry? You are being serious! Then, why do you call him nice? A king-to-be who doesn't even know the people who belong to his kingdom and who will only marry a princess? Like seriously? Stop admiring him now. Thanks for reminding me why this era is long gone. I can see that he is someone who wouldn't have any time to visit and know his own people in his own kingdom." Doris thought the customs that were popular back then were strange.

"I am sure that the era you live in now must be far better. However, this is how things work around here and in the other places I know about. And there is a little explanation for it. For example, marriage with someone of the same status helps with the compatibility of the couple. Imagine a princess married to a peasant. How would she be able to leave everything she was raised with? Perhaps being in love helps you spend your life together, but no parent wants their children to go through the miseries they might face through incompatibility or by way of their status or background being dissimilar. Now, similarly, since I am not educated like the royal women, imagine if I were to support a king in the future to run a kingdom. I may not do it as well as a real princess can. Because she must be brought up that way," Christine explained.

"You seem pretty fine to me and like you could support anyone. How difficult could it really be to support a king?" Doris may not have known the struggle life could bring to someone who ran a place, as she was quite young and privileged herself to have even known the struggles of common people in her own era. She watched too many princess movies, in which stories were just about the glamour and riches the characters in them enjoyed.

"You are funny. Trust me, it takes a lot to run a place. And about that support part, thank you for saying so. But truly, it is not about me. This is why these customs are built and are being followed. A lot is involved in a royal marriage, including benefits for nations, either to end a long rivalry or for some alliances. Or it could mean a lot more than I am aware of." Christine was quite understanding and mature for her age.

"But it is a marriage, not a business or a treaty," Doris observed.

"So, marriage is a treaty for the royals. You get lucky if you fall for the same person. However, I think you see the point of how they compromise their lives, to begin with. And so, there may not be any future for me with him. It is not as easy as it seems, sweet girl. I hope someday I can get over the emotions I have for him at the moment." Christine rested her case.

Doris created a bad image of the prince in her mind, but Christine had an explanation for everything. So, Doris didn't say much against him.

Christine had at least opened up and shared her thoughts about the prince. She used to be so alone after all and never had much time in her daily busy routine to interact with anybody after her mother was gone. So, she spoke her heart out and shared her feelings about her Prince Charming for the first time with someone. She was a teenager like Doris, and like every teenage girl, she had big dreams, wishes, and strong emotions too.

Doris also thought about someone. She now felt a little sympathy for the young man she had met in the forest. She smiled at their totally confusing conversation and at her own stupidity. She wanted to apologize now for her behavior and felt something so very nice that night that she forgot she was far away from her home.

Christine also met someone to share her feelings about everything she had in her heart. They chattered too much over dinner and slept late at night. Strange, but girls become best friends too fast. And in a similar way, they become each other's enemy too. It all depends on their way of taking things and their moods.

Chapter 7

The Prince

*T*he young man who had met Doris in the forest entered a castle.

His mother walked toward him, knowing that he had returned. "Edward! Where have you been? Oh my God! You are *bleeding*! You are hurt! I told you earlier only to go with guards, but who listens to me here? Oh, it must be *painful!* Someone … bring some bandage! And call the physician! Quick!" she shouted. "I shall teach them a nice lesson! I mean they know that you are a prince. How could they leave you alone? And tell me, where did you go? And how did you get this nasty wound?" his mother, who was the queen, inquired.

"Mother! Take a breath. Do not worry. It is just a small injury. I fought a bear to save a girl," Edward told his mother.

"What? What were you thinking? Is this whole thing a play for you? You fought a bear and … for a girl! Have you lost your mind? And what did you think? That I would admire or adore you for this ridiculous act? Do you not know how dangerous all these things are? When will you learn that you are our only prince? Your life is too precious for this kingdom and foremost for me?" Edward's mother scolded him with concern.

Two guards helped Edward walk into his room following the queen.

The royal physician came to see Edward. "See what has happened to him. Do you know our prince is returning from a fight with a bear?" His mother taunted him in front of the physician.

"Oh Mother, when will you realize I am not a small child anymore? Stop worrying about me. I am a grown-up now! Besides, every future king must be strong enough to handle situations like this. I cannot possibly depend on our guards for everything, can I? Also, I do not intend to be entirely dependent on our guards for my safety. I should be able to learn self-defense," he tried to explain.

"Very well, then. I will stop worrying about you!" she said. "Lord Fitzgerald!" the queen called their ealdorman.

"Yes, Your Majesty?" Lord Fitzgerald came forward, bowing in respect.

"Now, it is your responsibility to take care of Edward," she said.

"Right, Your Majesty," he replied.

"But Mother! What are you doing? Did you not hear a thing I just said?" Edward didn't want this.

"Yes, my child! I did hear you. It is a good thing that you wish to be independent and want to take care of yourself. It is gallantry. However, that very same thing caused you this injury, and God forbid such actions cause you your life!" the queen said.

The prince wanted to defend his statement while the physician checked his arms. "But Mother—"

"You asked me not to care about you. So, I shall now not worry about you! Lord Fitzgerald is going to take care of you. Right, Lord Fitzgerald?" she interrupted Edward and asked, looking at Lord Fitzgerald.

"As you command, Your Majesty," Fitzgerald replied, bowing again.

"Mother, I am certain that Lord Fitzgerald has better and more important things to attend to. Do you not, Lord Fitzgerald?" Edward did not want this.

"You are most important in my work, my prince," Fitzgerald replied.

"Very well. So, it is settled. Lord Fitzgerald, see that he does not go to the woods again, especially alone. I hope I have made myself quite clear," she ordered.

"Yes, Your Majesty," Lord Fitzgerald affirmed.

"I have bandaged him and given him a potion. The scratch is luckily not that deep. He shall recover in no time. His wounds will heal soon. Now, please allow me to leave, Your Majesty," the physician reported to Edward's mother.

"But Mother—" Edward tried to say something.

"Get some rest, my dear boy," his mother interrupted.

The queen, along with Fitzgerald, came out of Edward's room, while a guard escorted the physician out.

"Never leave him alone, Lord Fitzgerald! He is your responsibility," the queen said and left.

"Yes, Your Majesty, I will not leave him … alone," Fitzgerald said, with an evil grin.

Edward lay on his bed, took out the cloth that Doris had tied around his arm, and stared at it. Love was sprouting in his heart for Doris. He had never experienced this feeling for any girl before. That day was the most beautiful day for him. All this while, he only met girls who ran behind him, knowing that he was a prince. For the first time, he saw the natural behavior of a girl that was unique. Doris didn't know that he was a prince, and he didn't want that to change. He wanted to see where this went. But he felt anxious, wondering if they would ever meet again in their lives. He thought about Doris the whole night and was overwhelmed that he had met her.

I Hate Kids

The next morning, Doris woke up in nice weather with a wide yawn.

Christine was already awake.

Doris went outside to find Christine feeding some grains to birds, and there was a huge flock of birds. A few rabbits, squirrels, and deer were eating there too.

Seeing this, Doris exclaimed, "What on earth!"

"Oh hey, Doris, you are up. Good morning," Christine greeted her with a wide smile, throwing some more grains from the earthen bowl she was holding.

"What are you doing? What is this?" Doris was scared seeing so many birds.

"Just feeding my friends. Are they not lovely?" Christine asked Doris, looking at them with love.

"You really have gone crazy living in the wild. What are you? Some Disney princess hanging out with birds and animals?" Doris questioned.

"Disney princess? Why do you think so? I have been here alone, so I made a few friends. And what is wrong with it? They love me back too. Do you not, my darlings?" Christine said, throwing more grains toward them and making weird expressions as if she was talking to small children.

One bird flew and sat on Christine's shoulder as a response to what she had asked.

"Look, they are my babies. Why do you not hold them, Doris? They will love you too." Christine offered the bird on her shoulder to Doris.

"Hmm, I probably have ornithophobia, which is the fear of birds by the way, so polite pass." Doris was a little afraid at that moment.

"You fear them? But why?" Christine was surprised that someone could be afraid of such innocent creatures.

"Why? Because I get scared when they flutter those wings. And good that you are wearing those gloves while touching them too. If I knew earlier that you touch these wild animals, I would have asked you to wear one myself," Doris replied.

"But why are you afraid of that?" Christine tried to avoid the topic of her gloves and asked Doris about her fear since she could not understand.

"I'm just afraid, okay? I don't have any particular reason for that. Plus, they smell bad." Doris didn't have anything to say to explain her fear.

Christine started to laugh and mock Doris by talking to those birds in a toddler's tone. "Aww, look, Dorish ish scared of you." She continued laughing.

"Very funny. You sound so evil right now, do you know that?" Doris replied in an annoyed tone, making a weird face, and walked towards the bushes. "Oh, the most difficult part of the day." She talked to herself while walking. Then she got ready, and they moved toward the market after Christine was done feeding the birds and animals.

Soon, the market was before them.

"Why is it so muddy everywhere? It is too stinky here," Doris complained right after entering the lively area that came after the forest.

"Hmm ..." Christine didn't know how else a place was supposed to be, so she didn't have anything to say.

"However, it is somewhat nice. Your time is nice in its own way. No noise, no pollution. It's really calm." Doris saw the market of that time. She watched people making things with their own hands and barely using any machines, without electricity, which was intriguing.

Then, she noticed an old lady in front of them with a small girl about eight to ten years old, holding her hand and approaching them.

"Oh ho, Christine, how are you, my child?" the old lady greeted Christine. "Who is this pretty girl with you? I have never seen her here before," she continued, looking at Doris with Christine.

"Good morning, Aunt! I am fine. She is my cousin, Doris," Christine replied.

"Cousin? But if my age has not completely taken over my memories, I am not aware of any other family members that you had except for us. Then, which cousin is this now?" The old lady caught her lie.

"Ah … I meant she is …" Christine realized that she should have thought this through and said anything but that. But now, it was too late, and she was too confused to back her reply now.

"Good morning! She meant that I am her friend … her best friend, and she treats me as her sister. That is why she introduced me as her cousin." Doris tried to save Christine.

"Oh, yes! I meant the same. She is my very nice friend and lives in a nearby kingdom," Christine continued.

"Nearby kingdom? But you have never gone out of this kingdom. How can she be your best friend?" The old lady was suspicious.

"Oh, my mother used to come with me to meet her and her mother in that cottage. We have never visited this market. We always used to return after meeting them. It's my first time alone here and in this market." Doris tried to make their lie more convincing. She was already very good at lying to save herself from her mother's queries, and this felt the same for her.

"Oh, I get it now. Well, pardon my investigations, as this old woman is Christine's godmother, and I am supposed to take care of her," the old lady introduced herself.

"Oh, no problem at all." Doris hesitated, because the lies she just told sounded quite stupid now that she found out the woman was Christine's relative herself.

"Well, we welcome you to our giant yet peaceful kingdom. I am sure you will enjoy visiting it!" The old lady knew they were not speaking the truth, but she still greeted Doris with respect, feeling glad to meet her.

Doris noticed that the little girl standing with the old lady was smiling, watching Doris. Doris stared at her crossly. The small girl got scared and hid behind the lady.

"Okay, Aunt. I am getting late for my shop. We shall talk later. Goodbye, and have a nice day." Christine took her permission to leave and moved toward her shop.

"Oh, that lady was such a freak! Who was she? Some detective or what? Why was she questioning us so much?" Doris asked, as she was never used to be interrogated this much about her life, except by her mother.

"Oh, no. You are taking her all wrong. She is very nice. She worries about me so much—that is why," Christine tried to explain.

"Oh … so, do I look like a monster or a ghost who would eat you?"

"No, that is not what I meant. She is a nice woman who was just trying to know who you were. That is all." Christine giggled.

"So, everybody around here is good and nice and as sweet as sugar. I guess all the bitterness came up in our time," Doris said in sarcasm.

"Haha … I am not saying that. It is just that I have never met a bad person yet. If I meet one, I will surely inform you." Christine winked.

"LOL, you have a serious problem there. You don't know about judging people. How could you be so innocent? Everyone can't be nice. It's not necessary!" Doris said.

"And similarly, everyone cannot be bad either. And why do you have to judge anyone anyway? If you talk and behave nicely, then everyone will be nice to you too. People behave with you the same way you behave with them. My mother used to say that it is just like looking at yourself in the mirror. You always see your face in it when you stand in front of it. It reflects you." Christine tried to make Doris look at it from a positive perspective.

"Oh, I had read these cheesy lines in one of my literature classes, but it's not practical, you know? What if it's not about your reflection? What if the person before you is behaving badly in the first place? What would you do then?" Doris was talking about some practical things according to her.

"Then what? You do not stop behaving according to the way you are. If you are right and polite, there is no one in this world who will not bend their knees in front of you! Remember that forever." Christine also had answers to every one of Doris's questions.

"Oh … too much sweetness. I think I'm gonna get diabetic," Doris teasing Christine.

As they were talking, they reached Christine's bakery. It was in a nice area on the side of the earthen road on a wide plot of land. Christine started her work as soon as they entered. The room was made of woods and stones, and the floor was made of stones. It was filled with the aroma of fresh muffins and pies. Christine was good at baking and so was in decorating the baked products with patience and love.

"Oooh ... so much to eat. And everything looks so delicious! May I taste some of these?" Doris cried in joy and was amazed to see such a variety of baked things at once.

"Yes, of course, you may," Christine offered gladly.

"Oh, I can't decide where to start," Doris said in excitement. "Oh, it's really delicious! The best thing about having a bakery is you can eat whenever and whatever you want." Doris spoke with her mouth filled with a cookie.

Christine was smiling at being admired while doing her work.

"Seriously, I can't believe you made this. It is so fine. And without any oven."

"Hmm ... I have an oven. It is right there. How do you think I cooked all of them?" Christine showed Doris the wood-fired clay-oven of the time.

"Okay. What I mean to say is without an electric oven or microwave, you cooked this stuff!" Doris could not imagine how it was to cook in that fire oven.

"What is a *my-crow-wave*?" Christine had not heard this word too before.

"Hmmm ... Let's not ask for the meaning of words you do not know. And I will try to avoid using them. What I was trying to say is I have never consumed such a delight before. You really have magic in your hands."

"Oh, thank you, Doris! I am glad you appreciate my effort." Christine was happy seeing her new friend enjoying what she had made. She was truly enjoying company.

Doris tasted all kinds of things Christine had baked and was full. "Hmmm ... I am so full. I must say there is something about you and sweetness. You are sweet. Everybody you meet is sweet, and even your profession is all related to sweets. I will definitely get diabetic staying here."

"What is *dia*—" Christine now wanted to know the meaning of this term.

"It means you get sick when you eat a lot of sweet," Doris explained before Christine could say the word.

"Good lord, am I making people sick?" Christine asked.

"Oh no, silly. Just too much of it causes this disease. You don't have to worry," Doris explained.

She then also sold a few things while Christine was baking. Christine taught Doris to cook a little. They were having a great time together as girlfriends.

"By the way, I was thinking—where do I get a clue about how to go back?" Doris wondered out loud.

"Why? You do not like it here?" Christine asked. She was a sensitive girl. In her solitary life after her mother's death, for the first time, she found someone to be with. She liked spending time with someone of her age and was hoping she would stay with her now.

"Oh, sweety, it's not that. I too have started to like it here. But I need to know exactly what has happened to me." Doris gave Christine a side hug. In fact, Doris had never felt this good emotionally, though not much time had passed since they were together. She had never been in such trouble before and knew that nobody would have helped her to the extent Christine had, even though she was so rude to her in the beginning.

"Yes. Of course, you are right. You should at least search for a way. You could look around," Christine said, understanding her.

"But … alone! I just can't go outside without you. I don't know what to answer people or what to do outside." Doris wanted company.

"Hmmm, I must apologize, Doris, that I cannot just go with you leaving everything here. This will all turn bad. Also, I must earn money for tonight's dinner." Christine tried to explain her situation to her. She was not rich enough to let her day's goods rot. She earned money for herself on a daily basis.

"Don't you have that much money to make dinner today?" Doris asked.

"No. We work daily to earn. And I also must collect money for the tax and give some to Lord Meredith. He is the owner of this place," Christine tried to explain.

"Tax? What for? And this shop isn't yours?" Doris asked.

"No, I hope you understand me. But do not worry a bit. Give the same answer we gave Aunt Adyren to the people," Christine said in a helpless manner.

"Aunt Adyren? The lady we met while coming? How is she your aunt if I am your cousin? Won't she find out?" Doris asked.

"You handled it quite well, saying that you were my friend. Do not worry so much. She bought it," Christine said.

"All right! Do your work. I'll try this then," Doris said.

Doris watched people and their busy lives. She liked that quiet and peaceful place but was missing her friends, parents, and the noise of her time too. Everyone there was seeing a new face. She moved forward, deep in her thoughts.

"Are you new here? I am seeing you for the first time here," the voice of a lady said from a shop not very far from where Doris was passing.

Doris hesitated. "Yes—"

"Oh, she is our Christine's best friend, Doris. She has come here for the first time. Am I right, dear?" the same old lady, Aunt Adyren, who was also standing there, interrupted Doris before she could say anything.

"Yes," Doris answered politely, noticing the old lady.

"You are still here? Where is Christine?" she asked.

"She is in her bakery," Doris replied.

"She may have her work. She is such a hard-working girl actually. Hope you don't mind her leaving you on your own! By the way, where are you headed alone?" the old lady started talking to Doris again.

"I am just visiting your town—I mean, your kingdom," Doris replied.

"Oh dear, Christine is so unbelievable sometimes. She left her best friend visiting this strange place alone! Can she not give one day to her friend?" the old lady asked in front of Doris.

"Actually, that is no problem at all. She has too much work to do, so I thought I would not bother her," Doris tried to explain on behalf of Christine.

"Oh then, it would be quite a bore for you to see this place alone. Why do you not go with Cherry? She will give you good company and not let you get bored," the old lady suggested.

"Cherry? Who?" Doris asked.

"She is my granddaughter. She is just eight years old. There she is, playing." Adyren pointed at her granddaughter.

"Oh, I'm fine alone. Let her play there. Look how happy she is there." Doris noticed that she was the same girl she had seen when she met Adyren and tried to refuse her company.

The old lady called Cherry from the same place. "Oh, you are too shy. Cherry shall accompany you without any trouble." Adyren thought Doris was shy.

"Oh, I just hate kids," Doris murmured in disgust.

"What? Did you say anything, dear?" the lady noticed Doris say something.

"I said that I just *love* kids and look how *cute* she is!" Doris said with a fake smile.

"Yes, Grandmother!" Cherry arrived.

"Cherry, meet Doris. You saw her and know her, do you not, my love? She was strolling here alone. Christine is too busy. So, dear, could you accompany her?" Adyren asked her granddaughter.

"Of course, Grandmother!" Cherry said with a huge smile, looking at Doris.

"Oh, too much sweetness," Doris murmured again, giving the girl a fake smile.

Cherry, of her own accord, held Doris's hand and gave her an innocent smile. Doris also in return gave her a fake smile.

They moved forward. Cherry kept talking continuously while walking, and Doris was making fake expressions to show she was paying attention. She was not at all listening to a word Cherry said, felt annoyed, and thought of ways to get rid of her. But Cherry did not realize that and kept talking.

And since Doris was not known for her patience, she suddenly shouted at Cherry, "Will you please keep quiet! Enough is enough! I have a severe headache! God!"

Cherry had never heard such a loud voice. She got scared and started crying loudly. But in no time, Doris realized what she did. "Oh, I am so sorry. I didn't mean it. Please don't cry." She tried to stop her from crying. She also noticed that people around her were looking. "Please be quiet! See, everyone is looking," Doris said in a very low tone.

But Cherry didn't stop. Doris now closed Cherry's mouth with her hand and held her. "I think she struck her foot at this stone over here. That's why she's crying," she said, facing the people with a smile. She ran from there, holding Cherry. She reached a silent place where there was nobody around, or that was what she thought. It was a huge plot of land with trimmed lawn and a few trees of great shapes as if a topiarist had shaped them. They were planted in lines and symmetry. Not far, there were stone statues, again arranged beautifully around a fountain with hedges and beautiful flowers. It was well maintained and was completely different from what Doris had encountered since the incidence. Doris didn't notice anything around and just came to that quiet place. She went under a tree and released Cherry, who was still crying. In that lonely place, her voice was louder. Doris was trying to stop her crying.

"Just stop sobbing, okay? I'll give you chocolates. Okay, pizza." Doris tried. *What am I saying? Chocolates and pizzas probably didn't exist back then or now*, Doris thought. "Oh God, please stop crying. I am sorry," she said politely.

But still, she cried.

"Oh, can't this girl just stop sobbing? First, I hate kids, and now, she is crying. Just shut your mouth! You are giving me a headache. Oh God!" Doris lost her temper and raised her voice again.

Suddenly, Cherry stopped crying and wiped her tears immediately.

"Oh, you finally stopped crying. I should have said this earlier," Doris said, with a bossy smile.

Then, she noticed Cherry looking behind her. She turned back and saw the same young man she had met in the forest with Maddox. He was with two other men, one in his early 40s and the other young in his late teens.

Edward was blissful seeing Doris again, and so was Doris seeing him.

"Hey, what are you doing here? Hmm … I am so sorry that I left you there like that in your injured state. You saved my life, and I left you there alone. Later, when I thought about you, I felt ashamed and sorry." Doris tried to apologize for her mistake.

"You thought about me? Really? What did you think?" Edward was happy.

"Do not flatter yourself." She was blushing too.

"Hm, Aunt!" Cherry tried to say something.

"What did you just call me? Aunt? How dare you call me Aunt? What do you think of yourself? You tiny creature," Doris rebuked her.

Edward smiled looking at Doris. Lord Fitzgerald was a little bit confused.

Doris turned toward Edward and continued, "Sorry I had a little hitch. Where were we? Oh, yeah … how are you now?" Doris saw a bandage tied to his wounded arm.

"Oh, I am fine now. Thank you for asking." Edward was glad.

"Hope it was not too painful." Doris was worried.

"Yes. I mean, no. This? It was just a scratch." Edward didn't want to show that it hurt.

"Okay. By the way, what are you doing here?" Doris asked casually.

"What a prince would do in his own garden," Edward introduced himself with great pride.

Doris then noticed a big castle in front of her. Then, she looked at the young man behind him and Fitzgerald. The young man with Fitzgerald was charming too, and since he had been holding the belongings of the prince, Doris mistook him for the prince. One more reason might have been that when she met Edward in the forest, he did not mention it then—although Doris didn't let him speak at all. But when do girls ever realize they have not let a boy speak in the entire conversation?

She immediately held Edward's hand, pulled him toward her, and whispered in his ears, "Oh so, this is your evil prince?"

Edward was surprised and confused to hear this.

"Yeah, he has the same villain-like face I imagined listening to my friend's description. He does not sound good to me," Doris continued.

"Who said that?" Edward asked.

"Oh, what will you do with the name of that person? And by the way, nobody has directly told me this. I concluded all these things from her description of him," Doris said. "And also, your prince looks like a punk."

"And who said that?" Edward asked her, smiling.

"Oh, this is my own recent opinion after seeing him," Doris said.

Edward just smiled, listening to Doris. Cherry was listening to their conversation and was getting uncomfortable, and Lord Fitzgerald was trying hard to listen to their conversation.

"But Aunt!" Cherry knew his true identity and wanted to warn Doris.

"Again! Don't call me Aunt. If you call me Aunt one more time, I'll just throw you in an oven. Do you get that?" Doris again told her off crossly.

Edward nodded at Cherry, signaling her not to say anything to Doris.

"What? Why are you interrupting me again and again? What is it?" Doris asked Cherry, irritated.

"I … I think we should go home," Cherry said, understanding the prince.

"If you want to go home, go. Don't irritate me. I didn't ask you to come with me anyway," Doris scolded her. Then, she recalled she was standing in front of a prince and moved toward the person she assumed to be the prince and Fitzgerald. "I beg your pardon, sire. Where are my manners? I didn't know you were the prince. In fact, I am new here. I was telling your—whoever he is—how lovely this place is. You must have put a lot of effort into creating and maintaining all of it!"

The man was confused but was still happy receiving respect like he were a prince.

"I think I should go now, sire." She tried asking for permission to leave.

"But …" The other man wanted to know exactly what was happening and wanted to correct Doris.

However, Edward signaled him not to tell her the truth.

"Were you saying something, Your Highness?" Doris asked the person she assumed was the prince. Then, "Am I doing it right?" Doris whispered into Edward's ear, still bowing.

"Oh, you are a natural," Edward whispered back to her.

"I … I was saying …" The young man couldn't think of anything to say after Edward forbade him from telling her about him.

"He … he wants to know your name and wants to say that your hair is beautiful," Edward interrupted.

Doris understood that the young man was cleverly trying to find out what her name was, pretending it was the prince's wish to know it. And to the person she assumed to be the prince, she said, "Doris. My name is Doris Wilson, Your Highness."

"Doris, such a beautiful and unique name," Edward said, looking at her.

"Thanks. By the way, I never asked yours." Doris also wanted to know the name of the young man, so she asked him.

"My name is Joseph." Edward took the name of the other young man Doris had confused as the prince.

"But …" Fitzgerald was totally confused now, and Joseph couldn't understand anything too.

"Oh, how impolite of me. You must think that I never asked your name. However, that is because I happen to know your name. Well, who would not know the charming prince of this beautiful kingdom?" Doris said to Joseph, and by saying this, she looked at Edward to ask for the name of the prince.

"Edward. His name is Edward," Edward whispered.

"Yeah, I knew it. What a lovely name." Doris smiled.

Joseph did not know how to react.

"And who is he? Looks like a villain from a movie to me," Doris whispered into Edward's ear again, looking at Lord Fitzgerald suspiciously.

"And he is Joseph's father, Lord Fitzgerald, our ealdorman," Edward introduced Lord Fitzgerald. He was enjoying Doris's honest feedback on people.

"What? Your father!" Doris felt stupid for calling his father a villain in front of him.

"Oh, it's so nice to meet you, Lord Fitzgerald." Doris felt embarrassed, realizing she was making fun of the father of Edward (who she assumed was Joseph) and bowed before Fitzgerald.

Edward also realized that he should have said "my father" instead of "Joseph's father," but Doris felt too silly to notice it.

"I think I must go now. I have a lot of work there, so goodbye." Doris felt embarrassed and left in haste.

"Goodbye, Doris," Edward replied.

"Goodbye, Your Highness," Doris addressed Joseph from a distance, waving her hand.

Joseph smiled. Doris held one of Cherry's hands and left the place.

"My prince …" After Doris left the place, Fitzgerald tried to ask Edward.

"Oh, Lord Fitzgerald, just leave it and forget it. You will never understand. Let us go. Otherwise, Mother will give us both a long lecture, and I am in no mood for that at least now. Let us go," Edward said and moved toward the castle.

"Oh, Edward, you made my son a prince before that girl, but soon, my son shall be the prince for real and I shall be the king before everyone," Fitzgerald muttered and laughed.

"What was all that about, Father?" Joseph asked his father.

"Nothing, Son. Just know that you can practice being a prince before that girl," Fitzgerald said, wrapping his arm around his son's shoulder.

"I liked that girl," Joseph said.

"You shall get everything you desire, my son. Just have patience until then," Fitzgerald said.

Chapter 9

An Argument

While returning, Doris knew how she behaved with Cherry, who would definitely not praise her to her granny. So, she tried to do some damage control so Cherry wouldn't say anything bad about her to her parents.

"So … how has everything been with me, Cherry?" Doris asked Cherry on the way back.

Cherry didn't say anything but just looked at Doris with wide eyes.

"What? Why are you staring at me like that? You saw that I am friends with the *prince*. And if you say anything wrong or bad about me to your parents, I'll complain about you to the prince and make him punish you. So—" Doris directly blackmailed her.

"I understand what you are trying to say," Cherry interrupted.

"Oh, so, you are not as dumb as I thought you are. Great!" Doris said.

An Argument

They reached Cherry's house. Seeing them back home, Cherry's granny came outside. "Oh, so, you have returned. How was it? I mean, did you like our kingdom, Doris?" she asked politely.

"Oh, it was really nice. Your kingdom is really calm, peaceful, and beautiful. And with Cherry, it felt more beautiful. Such a sweet granddaughter you have." It is obvious by now that Doris employed her lying tactics again and again to appease the aunt.

Aware of the truth, Cherry only stared at Doris.

"Oh, thank you. My Cherry *is* nice—I know it. She likes guiding people and talking and helping others. However, you are a great soul yourself. That is why you are acknowledging that," the old lady said.

"RIP, logic," Doris muttered.

"Did you say something, my dear?" Adyren asked.

"I said thank you. You are so sweet. I hope she enjoyed my company as much as I did. Did you not, Cherry?" she asked, staring at Cherry.

"Yes … yes. It was really nice. I enjoyed her company a lot, Grandmother," Cherry said, frightened.

"Then, this is nice. You have both become fine friends here. Do visit us too, Doris." Cherry's granny didn't know the truth.

"Of course. Why not? I'll keep coming here. But for now, I should go. Christine will be waiting. So, allow me to leave." Doris didn't want to visit them again though.

"All right, dear. Goodbye," Adyren said.

"Goodbye, Aunt," Doris said. "Goodbye, Cherry."

"Ah, bye," Cherry responded, hesitating.

Doris left that place.

"Oh God, she was so irritating. She ruined my whole day." Doris was aggressively talking to herself on her way back and, with that thought, reached Christine's bakery.

"Hey Doris, you are back. I was regretting leaving you alone. I should have at least accompanied you on your first day. I was worried about you. Did you find any way back to your home?" Christine was relieved to see Doris back sound and safe.

"Oh, my mouth hurts from smiling at everyone and everything all day, without any reason. And don't you ask about my way back. Your aunt … she sent her tiresome granddaughter with me. I can't handle this. I'm calling her cotton candy from now on," Doris complained.

"Cotton candy?" Christine couldn't understand but giggled.

"Oh, that's a candy only made of sugar. And no doubt, she looks like one. Irritating people … and that tiny creature! I mean, how can a person talk so much? Had I not stopped her, she would have killed me by talking, or I would have killed her with irritation," Doris said, expressing frustration.

"Well, I'm afraid I do not think she is that talkative. She is so adorable. Why did you get so—" Christine tried to praise Cherry.

"Oh, that chipmunk now! Please stop admiring her. Let's go home. I have a headache. You were not there. And please don't make me meet anybody else. I can't smile anymore." Doris was tired of showing kindness and manners, which were all artificial to her.

Christine also knew that there was no use saying anything to Doris, so she quietly closed her bakery. They carried some utensils, bought something raw to make dinner, and moved in the direction of their cottage in the forest.

While having dinner, Doris started talking about whom she thought was Edward.

"I met your prince today by the way," Doris told Christine.

"Really?" Christine was full of enthusiasm listening to that. All the tedium she felt from the long, busy day vanished all of a sudden.

"Oh my God, look at yourself. You are so into him," Doris teased her.

"No, Doris. I am just happy to know that you saw him," Christine tried to explain.

"Well, I am sorry to say this, but he looks like a punk to me," Doris said, being honest.

"Meaning?" Christine didn't understand what Doris was saying.

"I mean he looks good, but it surely seems as if he has been pampered a lot from the beginning and doesn't know anything. You expect him to rule a kingdom! He was so blank. LOL, if Kate and Cyril were here, we would have given him a tough time. Total jerk! On the other hand, his alderman's son Joseph—my God, he is unimaginably charming. He looks like a prince from a fairy tale a girl would dream of. Edward is such a bore, and he …" Doris opined.

Christine was listening to everything Doris was saying. However, she couldn't listen to more criticism against the prince. She was a patient girl, but suddenly, she lost her temper. "Have you gone insane, or do you have some problem with everyone you meet?" Christine completely changed.

"I'm only recounting what I saw. I am not saying that the prince is ugly or whatever. I am just saying he is not fit to be a king. He looks like he wouldn't even survive without a bunch of knights. He seems too delicate and blank to be a future king. I know you are into him, and I am not saying he is not good as a person. I am just saying he doesn't appear fit to be a prince. I expected Edward to be better than Joseph. I sincerely wondered how a person better than Joseph would be! But honestly, I was so disappointed. And I was right to think that no one could match Joseph. And it makes me wonder how you could have such a huge crush on him when Joseph is also around." Doris tried to explain what she had seen.

"It is not because I am into the prince. I know the prince. In fact, every girl in this kingdom just swoons over him—and not only in this very kingdom. Princesses from faraway kingdoms too drool over him and wish to marry him at any cost. And you are comparing him with Joseph! You definitely sound like you have gone blind. Not just by looks, Joseph stands nowhere near our prince in terms of anything—name, talent, horse riding, sword fighting, courage, character, nature, manners, or kindness. He is just too perfect as the future ruler. No man can have all of it within, but he is the only man I know of his kind. And trust me

Doris, he is a dream," Christine said all of this without taking a breath.

Well, Doris never expected to see this version of Christine. The sugar syrup turned into a bitter gourd in a moment. But how could Doris refrain from saying anything in an argument? She was waiting to return to her true form anyway.

"Seriously? Edward? All the princesses who drool over him seem blindfolded then. It is just because he has the tag of a *prince*. And what is the need for getting so offended? For a moment, I thought, *Oh, you sweet Christine, your love is so pure, like from a fairy tale.* But I didn't know that in fairy tales, Prince Charming is charming just because he is a prince. Now, I see that it's mere greed. And your prince looks like some punk to me," Doris, being a blunt person, said whatever came to her mouth.

However, they were both having a dispute over the same person. So technically, they were on the same side, yet were fighting. The only problem was that Doris knew him by another name.

"All right, then. I am greedy, and therefore, I just do not wish to hear anything bad about him. Is that clear?" Christine was infuriated, and saying that, she left her table, jumped into bed, and entirely covered herself with her quilt, without finishing her supper and leaving it all at the table while Doris was still eating.

"Fine! Don't eat. But it will not change the truth that your prince is wicked, and you are greedy," Doris continued taunting.

"Oh, yes? Am I greedy? Guess who is doing the dishes tonight? You!" Christine said in response, first pulling the blanket off her face and covering it again.

"What? Why should I wash your dirty dishes? I am not your servant!" Doris said, amazed.

"Well, guess what? Neither am I. And I am not a fool who is letting you stay at my house, giving you food and facilities free of cost without any help, and allowing herself to be treated like this. And if you want to be here, you must do them." Christine was quite enraged.

"Oh, so, that's the real you. That was going on within you. You call this mere hut a house?" Doris was being thankless in anger now too.

"Oh so, find one. I know you are never thankful for anything anyway," Christine spoke the truth and covered herself with her blanket again to sleep. Since she had not fought with anyone before like this, it made her cry. But she hid her face within the quilt.

"Yes, I will. I don't need to live here anymore," Doris said, standing, and saw Christine didn't ask her to stop. Doris was really surprised at hearing such words from Christine. Christine's mirror theory really started to be proved. She spoke the same way Doris always did. She also saw the blind love Christine had for the prince.

"I am really leaving," Doris said but received no response. She, having too much self-respect, made up her mind to never return to Christine's place. Angrily, she opened the door to really leave. The sudden chilly breeze of the night, the darkness outside, and the scary sounds of animals made her realize that Christine was somewhat right about her doing so many favors without any appreciation from her. She stood quietly because she hadn't forgotten that cold night outside the house.

She also knew that Christine's words were bitter but true. Who would have allowed a stranger to stay at their place for such a long time? Also, even though Doris was aware that Christine liked the prince, she was insensitive to her. She took the wooden bucket and went outside to fill water from the brook. The weather was unpleasantly cold outside. She entered the small kitchen and kept the bucket beside the dirty utensils. She didn't even know how to wash them.

"Hmm we have a dishwasher at home but no point thinking about that. I have seen our maid doing the dishes sometimes, though. What's the big deal! I should take some dish soap in the scrubber and scrub the utensils. But dish soap? These things were not there during this time. Oh gosh, this is the height of punishments. Now, how am I supposed to wash these dishes?" She was talking to herself. Then, she saw some fibers and ashes in a bowl. "Oh, this is the way people back then used to wash utensils." Doris was a little bit happy now to have figured something out on her own. Then, she dipped her hands into the bucket to take out water but shivered. "Oh! Now, this water! How cold it is! If I wash the utensils with this water, I'll freeze to death, and if I do not wash them, Christine will throw me out of her house. Oh God, what kind of days are you showing me? I must boil the water a bit and then wash."

Then, she poured all the water from the bucket into the big earthen pot hanging over the hearth. The charcoal was still hot and red.

"Now? I forgot there were no lighters or matchsticks! Does it mean that I have to do that tribal kind of thing—rubbing stones to light a fire? Yeah, seeing the condition, I think it means the same," she muttered to herself.

She put some wood logs where there were ashes and red-hot charcoal, but it only gave out smoke. She started coughing, and her eyes turned red and filled with tears. She tried to rub and blow into it, but even that created nothing but smoke. "Oh, and I thought being grounded sucked!" It was a big thing for her, as she had never lived like this before.

Then, suddenly, her eyes fell on a burning candle.

"You got to be kidding me! The candle is burning there, and I am blowing at ashes like an asthmatic patient here. So silly of me! She then burned the wood logs with the help of the candle and heated the water. After that, she tried to pour the water back into the bucket, but the water was much too hot, and the pot was too heavy to handle. She couldn't pour the water, so she took a stone and broke the pot at its bottom. She then collected the water in the bucket and started washing the utensils. "Oh … it's stinking. Yuck! What the hell is this thing?" After all, Doris was doing the dishes for the first time, so it was a terrible experience for her. However, she finally did it. When she stood up, she noticed the flicker of the candle.

"Oh, no. No, no, no! Keep burning, please …"

But the last candle died.

An Argument

"Oh, that stupid candle. Couldn't just wait for two more minutes! Oh, where were Faraday, Tesla, or Edison at that time? I mean, this time."

It was dark all around. So, she carefully walked in the dark and somehow reached the bed.

In the castle, something fishy was going on. Fitzgerald was trying to bring the royal guards to his side.

"Dear mighty knights, the safety of our kingdom is in your hands. You are the great strugglers who are ready to give your lives whenever needed. I am afraid to put it this way, but you are all fools. I mean you are all too naïve. You are not aware that our king takes advantage of you without paying you well for your honesty and hard work. Although he is a king, without you all, he is nothing. We are the ones who give the king his strength. And what does he give us? Nothing! A small amount of money for our duties, loyalty, and devotion to him and his own kingdom! You even have no right to do whatever you want. And believe me, he will not allow you to do as you please if you want to in the future. He does not understand your feelings, your emotions. Even our dear prince is the same. He is quite charming and innocent indeed, but these things do not make a person a king! If he were to be the king, he would also be the same. He would only think about himself and his family and not about us—"

"I am sorry to interrupt you, Lord Fitzgerald," the baron said, "but we do not think so. He is kind and generous beyond what you know. Our king does a lot for us, and we can even give our lives to him whenever he needs them." The baron looked

Fitzgerald in the eyes, moving close to him, trying to understand his intentions, and kind of taunting him by taking the king's side.

"*Give our lives to him …*" Fitzgerald repeated his worlds to mock him. "Emotions and generosity do not get a place running, Lord Cai. He does not let us take proper taxes from the people. The treasury is depleting at an alarming speed on account of the *generosity* on his part that you mention. He does not let us fight for our own lands, fearing for the lives of his subjects. You are aware of how much land we have already lost to other kingdoms because of his fear. I know that he cares for us, but he is weak! If this continues, we will be left with nothing in no time. Our mighty kingdom may not exist in the future if I am not exaggerating. We need proper wealth to strengthen our army. Nevertheless, the king keeps donating it all to his people and thinks he is doing good."

"Do you think that I am trying to agitate you all to rise against the king? I am just trying to be kind toward you and warn you about what our future will be like. A kingdom needs a strong king who can make difficult decisions. Softness will only bring extinction to a nation. Someday, some other kingdom will attack us and take all that is ours. Each time, our boundaries cannot be bought by treaties. So, the choice is yours: wake up and try to act of your own volition or blindly follow the king," Fitzgerald said, angrily at first but calming himself down in the end.

"Yes, you are right! It is hilarious though that you mention this. However, interestingly, I agree with you on this. He should be careful with the extra generosity he shows to some ungrateful people … who rose up to the zenith from nothing and then

An Argument

dared to speak against him. Tell me, Fitzgerald. You of all must share that experience with us. What was it like, or have you forgotten your days so soon?" The baron spoke in favor of his king, coming close to Fitzgerald and making eye contact again as he smelled something burning inside Fitzgerald. He then ignored it, thinking that the king might have said something to anger him and that he may have taken it to heart. The baron tried to explain to Fitzgerald on behalf of his king. "Anyway, I will forget what you just said if you vow that you will never think about it again. Do not mistake his kindness for weakness. You do not know how powerful kindness and generosity are. It takes courage and selflessness to carry that out. He *is* a good king. Have faith in him, and you shall see."

Fitzgerald felt extremely embarrassed and angry too, because the baron said things against which he could not say anything. He understood that the baron was not at all ready to listen and follow what he was trying to say. Further, he realized he would not let him do his work, so he thought of doing something foul with him first.

An Invitation

The king was enjoying his breakfast with the queen on a fine morning in the sun at his lavish garden.

Edward joined them.

"How is everything, Son? I hear that you were attacked by a bear. How are you?" The king wasn't present when it happened.

"Oh, it was nothing, Father. Sometimes, it is worth having some wounds," Edward replied with a smile.

"Well, you look different … in a good way." The king pointed happily.

"Er … what change do you see?" The prince was a bit surprised to see his father was able to discern this fact about him.

"Oh, my boy, work keeps me occupied but not so much that I will not look out for my son and know when he is happy or sad".

"Oh Father, you are the best." Edward was mesmerized.

"You are my first priority, Edward".

An Invitation

"Father ... I have a question."

"Yes. Anything, my boy."

"Do you think I will be able to become a perfect person like you? Like, you are a loving husband, a fantastic father, and a perfect king altogether," Edward praised.

The king chuckled at Edward and answered, "You will be a far better person than I am, Son. Because you have my brain to run this kingdom, you're a fine warrior, and you have your mother's beauty, sense of fun, etiquette, talents—and what's foremost is that you have a beautiful heart of your own. Why would you doubt that?"

"I am afraid I won't be able to manage everything so well like you do, Father. You keep everyone happy," Edward replied.

"Oh look, Ffion. Our son sounds like a grown-up man now," the king said to the queen.

She smiled.

"You do not need to be so afraid, Edward. You will learn everything when the time comes, and moreover, with the help of a perfect queen, it should not be so difficult at all. I was not good at it in the beginning either, but your mother was quite some help," the king tried to explain to Edward.

"Then, how did you impress Mother? What was your story?" Edward was curious.

The king laughed and replied, "Impressing your mother was the toughest of all the tasks I have ever undertaken. She was so different from all the princesses I had ever met or had been introduced to. I met her at my best friend's wedding. She was the bridesmaid. I kept staring at her like a madman the whole time, and your mother was unaware of my existence. Every prince had his eyes on her. I was searching very hard for words to begin a conversation with her, and trust me, suddenly, I could not feel my brain. Nothing came to mind.

"Then, I told my friend, and he did me a favor by introducing me to her. Somehow, I managed to gather words to talk to her—like about the wedding, the bride, the groom. But still, I could feel that I sounded silly. I was the best man of the groom. Fortunately, I had the chance to dance with her, and that made me fall in love with her even more. I did not want that dance to ever end. But it did. I felt terrible about going away and wondered whether we would ever meet or be that close again.

"Then, on the day we had to leave, we went for a stroll in the garden and talked for a while. She asked me to be in touch, and when it was time to leave, she looked all around to check whether anybody was there, kissed my cheek, and just ran away. I was surprised by it and equally happy. I had never expected it. But I was feeling low that it was going to be goodbye, but she took that sorrow away with her. I then started writing to her, and eventually, she started feeling the same for me. We told our parents and got happily married."

Edward listened to all of this with rapt attention and felt wonderful about it. The queen was mesmerized too, listening to that story again and blushed. The family was enjoying this conversation.

"How beautiful! When did it occur to you that you love him too, Mother?" Edward asked his mother.

"Well, when your father said that I was completely unaware of his existence, that was not entirely true. I was watching him too. He was a true gentleman and was as handsome as you are now. How can a girl not fall for him? And I shared his feelings too when we danced. It was magical. The way he looked at me made my heart skip a beat. That moment made me fall in love with him. I realized it when the dance was over. I was thinking about him the whole night. It was all very natural. It is true that you cannot make someone love you, but you cannot stop yourself from falling in love with someone either. It all happens on its own. When it was time to leave, I did not feel good as well, and it's funny that I could feel he was not happy about that either. And the idea of him being sad was a devastating feeling. So, I started a conversation with him, and before going back, I kissed him and ran away so he would know that I loved him and wanted *us* to continue," the queen recounted her part of the story by placing her hand on top of the king's.

The king and queen looked at each other with love. Fitzgerald was standing right beside their chairs and was making faces, listening to everything.

"Ahem … ahem. Okay, I will leave you two for a while." Edward saw his parents and felt happy for them.

"Wait. Where are you going?" the queen asked.

"Er … nowhere," Edward answered, smiling.

"In that case, I have a question for you too," the king said.

"Oh yes, Father. Anything."

"Who is the lucky girl?" the king asked.

"What?" Edward didn't expect that. The queen was surprised too.

"Thank you for the wonderful conversation. It made me realize what the good change was about," Edward's father said.

"Oh my God, do we know her? Is she a princess? She must be a princess." His mother wanted to know too.

"I do not even know her much. I do not know who she is. However, she is indeed different from all, like you said Mother was. I suddenly feel happy. She talks so much. She does not even know that I am a prince, and I do not know where she is from. She is not from our kingdom though. She said she was lost. I did not have a good start with her either. She was in a hurry both the times we met," Edward told them about her.

"Great, then. What else do we want?" his father said.

"But she does not know me at all. And she keeps running away from me. I am not sure if we will ever meet again. And I know she did not like me much," Edward said, losing hope.

"Oh, that cannot be true. Do not think that. I do not know her, but I know you. And *no one* can stay without loving you. I hope you see her again and bring her to meet us soon." The king comforted him.

"Thank you, Father. I love you so much. You are the best indeed." Edward felt very happy and hugged his father with joy.

At Christine's cottage, in her sleep, Doris heard someone screaming her name. She woke up, startled, and realized that it was Christine, so she rushed to the kitchen from where the voice came.

"What happened?" Doris asked, concerned.

"What did you do last night? You broke the only cooking pot I had. In what will I cook now?" Christine was disappointed.

"Oh God, I thought some bear attacked you." Doris was relieved.

Christine glared at Doris for not answering her.

"Okay, I was unable to tilt it to pour water into the bucket without incident. But I did the dishes," Doris tried to explain.

"But you broke the pot!" Christine still complained.

"What's the big deal? We will buy another one for you. Jeez, Mom." Doris said.

"Buy a new one? Do you think I own a pottery shop?" Christine asked.

"No … But I said, 'We will buy another one.' And by that, I mean we will pay for it. And since you were the one who asked me to wash those utensils, you are the one who should be guilty." Doris tried to deflect the blame toward Christine.

"I asked you to wash the utensils—not break the pot! And I do not have so much money that you can break and destroy things here and I will keep purchasing new ones," Christine replied.

"Oh, come on. I'll pay you back every penny when I find my way back home. So, don't get mad at me. You're getting so annoying now." Doris thought Christine would appreciate her washing the utensils.

"I'm annoying?" Christine asked.

"Yes. And you are such a mom," Doris added.

"And you are worse than a three-year-old kid!" Christine replied.

"Oh, shut up! I'm not talking to you." Doris was frustrated.

"Oh, so you have been talking to the air lately. Do you know people like that are called mad?" Christine teased Doris. Basically, she was also behaving like Doris now.

"I think you are right. I am crazy 'cause I'm talking to you," Doris said.

"Fine," said Christine in anger.

"Yeah, fine …"

"Are you both fighting?" a voice asked, and Christine turned and saw Cherry's grandmother standing at the door of their kitchen.

"Oh, good morning, Aunt! What made you come here? Is everything fine?" Christine greeted her cordially.

"Good morning, my dear. Everything is fine. It is Cherry's birthday in a week. I have come to invite you both to join us."

"Oh … yes, I remember. And I will make her a nice cake like always," Christine said to Cherry's grandmother.

"We will be glad to have you both," Adyren said.

"Sure, I will be there." Doris replied.

"Were you two fighting?" Cherry's grandmother repeated her unanswered question.

Doris and Christine looked at each other and replied, "Yes."

"And may I ask why?" Cherry's grandmother asked.

"No, you may not." Doris was annoyed enough to put up the good girl act that moment, so she got rude.

"She means she broke my only pot last night, in which I *used* to cook. And I am left with nothing to cook my meals in," Christine complained.

"But she didn't even notice that I, *a beautiful girl*, did all the dishes on such a murderously cold night," Doris complained too.

"Oh, I am so honored by that." Christine had learned to emulate Doris's sarcasm.

"Well, you should be." Doris had an answer for everything.

"Will you please stop fighting? I just asked you for the reason of your fight—not for a demonstration," Adyren scolded them both. She continued looking at Christine. "And Christine, what has happened to you? I am sure she did not do it intentionally. You never quarrel, and now, you are arguing with your own best friend! It is very shameful."

Watching Christine getting scolded, Doris started smiling.

"See? That was so easy for you to understand. I was trying to tell her the same," Doris said to Adyren.

"You should not be fighting too, Doris. She is your best friend as well, as both of you have told me. Is this the way you both fight daily? Because my definition of friends is quite different." Adyren crossed-examined Doris as well. "I do not think that this reason made you both quarrel because I know Christine so well. However, whatever the reason is, I advise you this since you are such good friends: nothing should come between true friends. Friends are sometimes the most important people. You share feelings with your friends that you cannot even share with your parents sometimes. These kinds of small quarrels get bigger with time if you keep them in your heart. You are both mature enough to understand whatever I am trying to say. So, let go of your anger and hug." She tried to resolve their conflict.

"Hug her? Is that really necessary?" Doris asked with a disgusted expression.

In reply, Adyren stared at her and said, "Of course."

"All right, all right. I was just kidding," Doris said, moving toward Christine to hug her.

Christine moved back to avoid the hug and looked at Aunt Adyren.

"Er ... or a simple apology should be appropriate too," Cherry's grandmother said, understanding Christine's expression and noticing that she was not wearing her gloves. Doris felt rather weird about Christine moving back to avoid the hug.

"My sincerest apologies, Doris. I do not know why I got so agitated. I am not like this truly," Christine said, looking at the ground.

"Ah, it's all right," Doris said in a casual way.

"Now, you too, Doris," the old lady said with a smile.

"Me? But why? What did I do? She started it." Apologizing was always a difficult task for Doris.

Cherry's grandmother looked at Doris.

"Okay, you win. I am sorry, Christine," Doris said in a forced manner.

"It is okay, Doris. It was my fault. I got angry unnecessarily." Christine really realized that it was her mistake.

"See, you are admitting!" Doris teased.

"Oh, you girls are impossible! Now, I am going. I hope you do not start fighting ever again in your lives. Friends are meant to help each other." Cherry's granny said goodbye and left.

"Oh, that old terrifying zombie—she just sucks!" Doris got irritated.

"Did you not listen to her? Now, help me bake muffins," Christine said.

"Muffins? Do you want your bakery to close after selling muffins baked by me?" Doris said, and both laughed.

"I shall teach you. Now, come on," Christine said with a smile. They both carried the required things like fermented dough, yogurt, fruits that Christine had plucked earlier for flavor, etcetera and moved towards the market. On the way, they bought some more things like milk and eggs that were required and reached the bakery.

Christine taught Doris to bake muffins there. Though Doris was new at it, she took an interest in being with Christine and helping her out. Helping others wasn't as bad as she thought it to be. They made breads and some more bakery products.

"Now, I am left with making cookies. Are you going to help me?" Christine asked.

"You'll make it? I thought all these things were made in factories or something like that!" Doris was amazed to see that the most basic things were hand made. She saw how much energy Christine was putting in kneeing the dough. How she had been shaping the cookies and how precise she was with her ingredients.

"What is a fact-tree now?" Christine asked.

"Never mind ..." Doris said to Christine.

"Hmm ... Doris?" It was Cherry at the big open window of the bakery calling for Doris.

"*What* are you doing here? I thought you wouldn't dare show me your face since the last time we met..." Doris said to Cherry.

"Hm ... *I* did not come here to call you. The prince—I mean Joseph is calling you." Cherry was a mere messenger.

"Joseph? What for?" Doris wondered out loud.

"I do not know," Cherry replied. "He is at the same place where you met him yesterday in the garden near the castle," she continued.

"You went to the royal garden yesterday? Why?" Christine asked, surprised.

"I didn't actually know that that was the royal garden. Cherry started crying, so I took her and ran somewhere where people were not watching to make her stop. Later, I realized that it was the royal garden. It was there that I met your prince." Doris told her what she couldn't tell her before.

"Oh," Christine said.

"Hm ... don't worry. I won't flirt with your prince." Doris winked at Christine.

"Now, what are you waiting for? Do you want to come with me? I am sure you don't want to, for your own sake. Then, why the heck are you still standing here?" Doris asked Cherry.

Cherry felt afraid and ran away from there.

Doris left to see her presumed Joseph.

"Good morning, my lady," said Edward chivalrously, taking her hand and kissing it.

Doris was flattered, but she behaved in her regular manner. "Oh yeah, good morning. Why did you call me? I have a lot of work to do. So, hurry."

"I ... I called to ask you ... Would you care to join me for a horse ride?" He hesitated after she responded in that manner.

"What? You really called me for this? Are you crazy? I'm going back." She started to walk away.

"Hey ... wait. Please do not go. I mean I feel so suffocated here. I do not have any friends over here. I want ... I *need* a friend. So, I called you." Edward didn't have anything better to say to make her stop.

The jerk is inviting himself to be friend-zoned, Doris thought. She knew that he was trying to get some time alone with her but was failing. She knew she didn't belong there.

"No ... you listen to me, Joseph. You don't know who I am or where I belong. You are not a kid who needs friends to play and pass time with. And the most important thing is I can't be your friend," Doris said to him.

"But why?" He wanted to understand.

"Because I am not of this time. I mean I don't belong here! I am here for a few days. Even I am not sure when I would have to leave." Doris tried to explain herself to Edward to avoid any heartbreaks.

"But until then, you could be my friend! I shall be really glad even to be your friend for those few days." Edward was trying his best.

"Can't you understand me? I know you people. I thought you were naïve, but you are not. You are just a flirt. I didn't know that people of your time also flirt." Doris couldn't think of anything else to avoid him too.

"People in my time? You are talking as if you are from the future! And by the way, I am a prin—I mean, the son of the ealdorman aiding the prince in the kingdom. So, girls are crazy about me. I do not need to flirt with anybody." Edward felt a little offended at her confusing replies.

"Then, this is your misunderstanding. Even though your prince looks like a total jerk, girls are crazy about him and not about

An Invitation

you! Oh, why am I wasting my time here? I'm going. Bye!" Doris found a way to exit the conversation.

Edward was a bit angry too, so he didn't stop her. His entire joyous mood after listening to his parents' story was ruined now. He was even surprised to see the way Doris talked to him. Although he was a patient man, nobody had ever spoken to him like that or ignored him each time after everything.

While returning, Doris recalled her conversation with Edward and smiled, which was totally confusing for both. She found love brewing for that stupid son of the ealdorman in her heart and was unnecessarily feeling happy and excited. A big, uncontrollable smile appeared on her pretty face.

On her way back, she noticed a small shop where she found pots. She remembered that Christine didn't have a pot, so she thought of helping her. As she didn't have anything else to buy it with, she took off the chain she was wearing and bought more than she had damaged. She bought some groceries and flowers for Christine along with the best cooking pot she could find. Being in love opened her heart to generosity. Doris felt good doing this. Her heart was thankful to Christine.

She was enjoying her thoughts when, suddenly, a ball hit her head and woke her up from her daydream. She found a few children standing and looking at her, waiting for her response. Cherry was also among them. She got angry and was going to respond in her characteristic way but noticed the people around her and behaved calmly instead. "Oh, what would be better than seeing children playing this fantastic morning? I love kids. Enjoy yourselves, little ones." She gave them a fake smile, looking at Cherry and throwing the ball back at her politely.

Cherry took no time to understand that if Doris found her again, she would definitely kill her.

Again, Doris walked, murmuring on the way to the bakery, "Freaks—I just hate kids! They spoiled my whole mood."

Christine was waiting for Doris and was curious to know what was cooking between her and Joseph. However, when Doris returned, she came back with a lot of stuff.

"What is all this? Who gave you this?" Christine didn't expect Doris to bring so many things on her own.

"What do you mean who gave me this? I bought all of them," Doris replied.

"You? Seriously! But how?" Christine was surprised.

"Oh, don't bother. On my way back, I saw this shop where they were selling these things, and it reminded me that we didn't have anything to cook our dinner in," Doris explained.

"Oh, Doris! That is very kind of you. You did not have to." Christine could not believe Doris could do something like that.

"Yes, I needed to. I have been staying with you and have not shown my gratitude so far. On top of that, I caused you trouble. So, here is my way of saying thank you and sorry," Doris said, extending the flowers she had bought.

"Doris, I do not know what to say! I am really sorry if I made you feel that you had caused me trouble. I went too far last night and

An Invitation

today's morning, and yet, you did such a kind thing in return!" Christine got emotional and hugged Doris.

"All right, all right. I think we're good." Doris didn't know how to react in such a situation.

"By the way, how did you manage to afford all of it?" Christine wondered about the obvious as Doris didn't have any currency of that time to buy anything with.

"Hmm, I was done with my necklace. It was old, and I didn't like it anymore. Also, I have plenty at home," Doris replied.

"Oh, Doris! I feel so ashamed that I said all those mean things to you last night that made you do this." Christine really was speechless at the gratitude Doris showed.

Christine wanted to ask her about her meeting with Joseph. But since she was still processing this, she kept it to herself for the moment. They continued their work and returned home at dusk.

But since girls can't keep anything in their stomachs for too long, Christine started throwing up her questions: "What happened there? Why did he call you? You can tell me everything if you want. And what did you two talk about? Did you—"

"Hey, one by one. Could you ask your list of questions one by one?" Doris was equally eager to share her feelings and her thoughts with someone. "He was trying to flirt, you know? Always, whenever he meets me, he does the same," she continued.

"What? Flirting? Doris … I am not sure of how to put this, but I am afraid that he has a fiancée." Christine told Doris about the real Joseph.

"Are you pulling my leg? I mean he can't have." Doris couldn't believe it because even though she didn't behave well for her own reasons, she was into him but would not admit it openly.

"Look! I want to see you happy and in love. The kind of love that changed you so quickly, in a good way. I really care for you and would not want anyone to break your heart. However, if you do not wish to believe me, it's better to ask him. You must ask him." Christine was so sure about what she had said.

Doris remained quiet.

Chapter 11

Christine's Secret

*I*t was Cherry's birthday. Christine had a lot of work at her bakery, so she, along with Doris, started her work early in the morning. She had to bake too many things for the celebration. Doris also helped Christine to her best capability and capacity.

It had been a few days since Edward had not seen Doris. Even though he was angry at her behavior when he met her last time, he still couldn't take his mind off her.

Adyren and Cherry went to the castle to invite the king, queen, and prince to Cherry's birthday, even though they knew they wouldn't come to their small house for a small celebration, like every time. Nevertheless, it was their duty to inform them. When they went to the castle, Fitzgerald stopped them at the door of the castle.

"Hey, old woman, what are you doing here?" Lord Fitzgerald asked.

"Oh, good morning, my lord. It is my granddaughter's birthday today, so I have come here to invite the king and queen to the small celebration we are organizing at our house. Oh, and I invite you too. We would be really pleased to have you at the celebration." Cherry's grandmother invited him even though she hated him for her own reasons.

Fitzgerald laughed at her in mockery and said, "What makes you think that I would come to the cheap birthday celebration of a filthy skunk? And what is funnier is that you dare to call His and Her Majesty to this!"

Cherry was very much offended, but her grandmother held her back from saying anything.

"What? Are you hurt, little skunk? Why were you even born? Look at yourself! You are pathetic, and you add hideousness to our kingdom. On top of that, you want to celebrate your birth! Better go back if you wish to be alive to celebrate your birthday in the evening." Fitzgerald took it too far.

Cherry's grandmother was turning back from there after being terribly offended. It was a pathetic thing to hear that being said about her granddaughter on her birthday. She could not do anything but clench her fist to hold her anger in and started to leave. But a voice stopped her.

"Hey, Cherry! How come you are here?" Cherry and her grandmother looked up the stairs to find it was the prince.

"Your Highness! Good morning!" Both Cherry and her grandmother bowed with respect to the prince. Fitzgerald was jealous out of his own sheer nature.

"Good morning. It is so good to see you, Cherry. What made you come here?" the prince asked.

"It is Cherry's birthday, my prince. We came here to invite you to our small celebration in the evening." Cherry's grandmother hesitated while saying this again, after being humiliated before.

"Oh, that is wonderful! Happy birthday, sweetheart! How old are you now?" Edward asked with great joy.

"Oh, I turned nine today," Cherry replied.

"That is great. Tell me—what would you like for a present?" Edward asked.

"Oh, nothing, sire. Your mere presence would be the biggest gift to me," Cherry replied.

"Oh, look how maturely you speak already. What makes you think that I won't come? I shall definitely come to the birthday celebration of my comrade," Edward said, winking at her.

"Really?" Cherry's grandmother was amazed and happy to know that the prince knew Cherry.

"Of course! Also, allow me to help you with the arrangements," Edward said.

"Oh, Your Highness, that is so very generous of you, but we do not want to cause any trouble to you. Truly," Cherry's grandmother said with great respect and joy at the same time.

"There is no trouble. You do not have any idea how much Cherry helped me. I at least ought to do this much," Edward said and turned toward Lord Fitzgerald, who was still standing there and listening to all of it. "Lord Fitzgerald, I want nice arrangements for the celebration. Take whatever and whoever you need."

"Yes, my prince," Fitzgerald said. He felt ashamed and angry, as he abused them before and said that he wouldn't be going. But now, he had to make arrangements at their place. This was completely degrading for him.

"Oh, my prince, that is too much trouble to give you. It was going to be a very small celebration." Cherry's grandmother hesitated.

"Oh, you are thinking too much. There is no problem at all. What are we here for anyway? It is our duty to keep our people happy," Edward said. It indeed won their hearts.

"I am so glad, Your Highness, that we are blessed to have you as our future king. God bless you, Son." Cherry's grandmother was overwhelmed.

"Thank you. I am learning from my father, you see," Edward said with a smile.

"Long live the king!" Adyren said with a smile.

"Long live the king!" Cherry repeated with her childish, adorable voice and a toothless smile.

When they started to leave, Edward stopped them to ask Cherry, "Hey Cherry, is Doris coming too?"

"I think so. Grandmother has invited her and Christine," Cherry replied.

"That is lovely," Edward said with joy. "But she must not know that I am Edward. You remember that, right?" he continued.

"Yes, Your Highness. I do," Cherry said.

"But why?" Cherry's grandmother couldn't understand.

"Because this is Cherry's and my little secret. Is it not, Cherry?" Edward asked, looking at Cherry and winking. "Please take care of it, would you?" he asked Cherry's grandmother to keep it this way as well.

"Anything for you, my prince," Cherry's grandmother said with a smile, and they left.

Fitzgerald obeyed the prince's command. Everybody noticed that royal servants worked at Cherry's place. Soon, the news spread that the prince was coming to their place. People were excited, and so was Christine.

"Oh my God! The prince will come to Cherry's birthday celebration! I can hardly wait for the evening. We need to look good, Doris." Christine was so excited.

"No, *you* need to look good. I am gifted with natural beauty already." Doris was least bothered, as she didn't know that the prince was who she thought was Joseph.

Christine didn't say anything, as she didn't want to look overexcited, which she was.

"I was kidding. You look absolutely beautiful too, Christine. Why do you worry so much? Your prince will not be able to take his eyes off you. Nobody here in your kingdom is as beautiful as you are. And I am not saying this because I am your friend but because it is true. I have met so many people, including in my time. It is difficult to find such a pretty girl. I don't want to say this, but when I first saw you, I was like 'Woah.' But since we didn't know each other and I was in so much trouble, I could not say it. Also, my focus was taken away by your attire, and you commented on my beach dress—why you did that makes sense now. Anyway, I wouldn't have spoken this way, but you really are the prettiest girl I know—although your dressing sense is horrible, which is not your fault again. I think people in this era follow the same dressing sense without any curves in their dresses as I have noticed, with which I can help," Doris said again.

Christine remained quiet, as she was clueless about Doris's references to fashion.

"All right, do not make that face now. What were you going to do when you said we had to look good?" Doris understood.

"Eee ... help me out," Christine said with joy again.

They finished their work quickly and then went back to their place. And now, this was the time for them to shine. Although this celebration was in their town, it was exciting at their age, and for Christine, it was not something that happened very frequently. Also, since she lived in the forest, she knew quite a bit about the plants and herbs that they could use to their advantage. She knew what smelled nice in the forest, what flower had the best color to be used, and so much more. So, she made up her mind to do her best and took charge of cleansing. She applied the ashes of burned vine to her and Doris's hair, boiled some chaff and sowbread, and poured some olive oil along with lemon peel to wash their hair with. To Doris's surprise, their hair looked really good and shimmered. They took a nice hot bath in rose water and milk. Next, they applied wheat bran as a face peel exactly how Christine guided. Then, they applied wheat starch as a face mask with natural beeswax and lemon. They hydrated their skin and looked radiant.

Christine plucked a few roses to make some color for their makeup. Also, she ground some lily root to whiten their complexion. Doris learned so many things and enjoyed this too. She also taught a few things, such as manicure and pedicure, to Christine. Doris helped Christine alter the dresses they were going to wear for good shape. Christine was reluctant in the beginning but soon realized how good the same dress looked with the changes Doris suggested. Then, Doris took up the styling of their hair. She asked Christine to let her hair lose, rather than cover it like nuns. They had a wonderful and graceful experience, getting ready in the traditional style. They both wore the best dresses and laces that Christine had managed to adorn the dress with herself. They looked gorgeous, and happiness brought an additional glow to their blooming faces. Christine was about to wear the gloves that she always wore, looking at which Doris said, "Oh no, no, no. Don't ruin it. Not today. You look so pretty, but this thing will ruin everything. Take it off today. I am sure your late mom wouldn't be angry for a day. She would rather be happy."

"It is not only about my mother, Doris. You do not understand. I cannot take it off," Christine said.

"What on earth is so important to make you wear that? It looks off with your new dress!" Doris wasn't feeling right about it.

Christine said nothing.

"Just take it off, Christine. One day. That's all I ask." Doris was after those gloves with her stubbornness, finally making Christine take them off.

Then, they both went to Cherry's place.

The celebration, expected to be small, was grand. Too many people gathered. Everyone was looking for Edward, and he did come along with Joseph and Fitzgerald with a gift wrapped in a red silk cloth. It looked huge. Whispering started. Everyone wanted to see what was in it. Joseph was carrying it, and they presented it to her. Cherry was the most excited of all. Why shouldn't she be? It was for her after all. When she removed the cloth, it was a big golden metallic horse. Everyone was amazed, and Cherry and her family were overwhelmed by it. It surely impressed Christine and Doris too, like everybody.

"Happy birthday, Cherry. This is on behalf of the royals to you, and they all wish you a very long and beautiful life ahead. This horse represents bravery, and may you get a Prince Charming on a horse like this," Joseph said all on the prince's behalf.

The prince smiled, standing beside Joseph.

"Oh my God, thank you so very much, my prince. I am out of words. This is the best thing ever gifted to me, and this is the best birthday ever. I feel so special." Cherry couldn't bear the happiness and had never imagined she would receive so much love.

"See, Doris. Did I not tell you that our prince is the best?" Christine said to Doris.

"All right, all right," Doris agreed because she was also impressed by this gesture. But her eyes were on Edward, who was Joseph to her. She simply felt nice, yet a bit hurt looking at him.

Edward looked at Doris and gave her a smile. He was a little disappointed at her before but felt excellent seeing her after days. Also, he felt that she looked gorgeous. He tried to go to her but noticed Christine was not leaving her side at all. People crowded around him so much that he could not reach her. They lit a fire outside at dusk and enjoyed the warmth and presence of the prince at their celebration. They danced around the fire, and Joseph stood next to Edward throughout as he had asked and enjoyed the celebration too. Fitzgerald was the only one who couldn't stand it. He just got green-eyed when people praised the prince each time. Doris was happy too. She was feeling wonderful there, and the weather, darkness, stars twinkling in the clear sky, beautiful decoration, perfect breeze, and warmth of the fire with people being happy and singing were just adding right to making her feel soft. And the softness somewhere was making her fall in love with Edward. However, the thought that he was getting married made her feel upset too.

Christine was happy too but looked anxious, as she was not wearing her gloves. People noticed this, as her gloves were something without which Christine never appeared in public. She was preventing people from coming close to her.

"Why are you acting so weird?" Doris whispered in her ears.

"Oh, nothing. I just have to help Cherry's mother arrange the food. Will you come along?" Christine asked, moving toward Cherry's house.

"Okay, sure." Doris went in too to avoid Edward.

Christine brought the cake she had prepared and beautifully decorated, with the help of Doris holding it at the other side. The cake was big and in three layers. Cherry reached out to Christine's hand to hold it with excitement, but Christine panicked and tried to avoid her, because of which the cake dramatically fell. Everybody looked at them and went silent.

"What the hell, Christine! What is wrong with you?" Doris shouted, holding only the plate as the cake was down on the floor.

Christine felt extremely embarrassed and ran toward her cottage. Doris also noticed the people around her and understood they ruined the party.

"Sorry, Cherry. I didn't mean for this to happen. Happy birthday," Doris said to Cherry and followed Christine.

Cherry started crying. Only Fitzgerald was more than happy now.

Edward consoled Cherry and said, "Is it really necessary to have a cake? We have everything else. Please continue."

The people also were mature enough to know it was an accident, so they ignored this incident and continued. But Edward did not feel the same when Doris left. Seeing Doris after many days made him fall in love with her more than ever. Also, she looked gorgeous. He wanted to talk to her but couldn't.

Christine reached home and was feeling awful about spoiling the cake and being embarrassed in front of all the people. Also, she had prepared it with all her heart since the prince was going to taste it too. She was feeling upset. Doris arrived and started to shout, "What the hell was that? I could see that you were acting strange. What is it?"

"It was an accident." Christine said in a very low tone.

"No, it wasn't. Though I can't stand Cherry, I can say that she was just going to hold your hand out of excitement, and you just didn't let her, and the cake fell. Tell me, Christine—what is the deal with touching you? I bought that lame explanation back then when you said it was because you like the gloves given to you by your mother and because of the wild animals you touch and all. But I have stayed here long enough to notice that it isn't about the gloves. You simply avoid people. I have faced it too. Spill the beans now. What is this about?" Doris wanted answers now.

"It is not so, Doris," Christine said, looking at the ground with tears filled in her eyes just about to fall.

"Oh, yeah? Then, prove it. Let me shake hands with you," Doris said, approaching her and extending her hand. But Christine started to cry. "No, no. You cannot touch me. No one can touch me."

"But why, Christine?" Doris asked, seeing her cry.

"Because if people do, they turn into statue," Christine said, crying loudly.

"What?" Doris couldn't understand.

"I am cursed, Doris. That is the reason I still live here in solitude, away from all the people, because the more people around me, the higher the chances that they will notice and the more queries and doubts they will have. That is the reason I wear gloves all the time when I go out in public to prevent them from being touched by me. I did it to stop Cherry from turning into a statue. I spoiled it all. I cannot be with anybody. Girls of my age are already married, except for me because I cannot. It does not matter, even if I liked somebody. I was not found near this brook but within the deep forest in the arms of a lady carrying me, I had touched her, and she had turned into a statue. My foster mother witnessed that, so she knew it all along. Yet, she took me and raised me as her own but had been careful since and had taught me to live with it. I touched a deer while conscious a few years back because I found it pretty, and it turned into a statue too. Nobody knows this except for Cherry's grandmother, because if the townsfolk learned of this, they would be scared and would never let me step inside the town. Nobody will like me, and everyone will call me a witch. And now, you will do that to me. I understand if you do not want to live with me anymore." Christine finally spoke her truth, crying.

Doris was surprised but could now understand it, as she had seen the broken statue of a woman the very moment, she entered the book. She held Christine's shoulder and said, "You have made me a better person, Christine. How could I do that to you? I am sorry I shouted at you without knowing your reason."

"But are you not scared of me?" Christine asked, wiping her tears.

"Why would I be scared of such an incredible and innocent soul?" Doris replied.

"But it is not safe to be with me, Doris. I am scared to death at the thought of turning Cherry into a statue. I will not forgive myself if it happens. And I cannot do that to you accidentally," Christine said.

"Oh, my sweet Medusa, don't worry about me. We have been living together for so many days. If it hasn't happened until now, it will not happen in the future. And I will not ask you to take that ugly thing off too and will be extra careful. Now, don't cry, and smile because I can't stand tears," Doris said, giving the gloves to Christine.

Christine smiled and felt better. "I wish I could hug you."

"Well, you will have to wear that ugly thing, and by then, that moment will go," Doris said, teasing her.

Christine giggled, wore the gloves, and hugged Doris. "Thank you, Doris. It is so nice to have you. I do not know how it would be if you were not here."

I Know the Story

The following morning, in the real world, Cyril brought a book to Katie. "Hey Katie, look!"

"What is it?" Katie asked.

"This is a book about the girl who had the curse of turning people into statues by her touch," Cyril told her.

"Is this story the one Doris has entered into?" Katie asked, surprised.

"I think so. I read it. It has the exact same story that is happening to Doris there, except that Christine stayed alone and the prince was in love with her—not Doris. I mean of course Doris did not exist back then. But Christine was reluctant to meet Edward for the fear of not belonging to that place, and she used to run away from the prince and sometimes purposely be rude to the prince, as she feared her curse, even though she always loved him. It is Christine's story. She was the one Edward had met in the jungle while plucking apples for the dessert that she made in her bakery.

She was attacked by the bear when Edward saved her. It was her for whom Edward asked Cherry to be called to meet him, and she avoided the meeting again—not Doris—because of her curse. But all of it is happening with Doris instead, with the twist or addition of the Joseph–Edward confusion. I don't know why that is happening though."

"Oh my God, where did you find it? And how do you know about such a story?" Katie asked, taking the book from him and flipping the pages to verify what Cyril had told her.

"I have lived my entire life with you girls and my sister. What did you expect? I saw my sister reading this a few days back. Yesterday, when we read about the curse Christine spoke about, it immediately hit me. But I was not sure, so I didn't say anything then. I had just noticed the picture on the binding the book had. It was of a girl touching a statue. I wanted to confirm, so I read it last night, and it has very similar events that are going on in this book. I thought that this must be some stupid fairy tale, but this seems real," Cyril elaborated.

"This is so great! At least we will have a clue now, and we will have an idea of how we can get Doris back. Oh, you are a genius, Cyril!" Katie said, kissing Cyril on his cheeks and hugging him in excitement.

There within the book, Doris woke up late, with the sunlight in her eyes.

"Good morning, Doris!" Christine was getting ready.

"Yeah. Good morning. You are not in the kitchen today, like always! Aren't you going to the bakery?"

"I am not sure. I do not feel like going at all. How will I face everyone? They all know how silly I was yesterday, and it feels like I will die of embarrassment. I, however, have finished all my work to go, but I am not sure what people will say!" Christine was obviously embarrassed at what had happened the day before.

"Oh, don't be an overthinker. Seriously, nobody cares. Accidents happen. There's nothing to be ashamed of. And I have seen that people around here love you. I think they can get over one 'cake dropping' incident by you. Although they would have thrown me out of their kingdom if it were me!" Doris said, giggling and trying to console Christine again. "Come on, don't let people's judgments keep you away from your work. And anyway, those people will not have a very nice day if they don't start it with your bread!" Doris continued to cheer her up.

"Okay, I definitely would not have gone if you were not there. I really would have stayed back at home. But okay, let us go and make their day sweet! So … are you coming with me?" Christine said, standing up with a positive attitude, all set to go.

"Hmmm … no. I don't want to go today. I don't know why I feel so lazy and tired. But if I feel like coming there, I'll surely join you. For now, I will sleep some more." Doris was exhausted from the work she had done the day before, which was unusual for her.

"Okay then, bye." Christine left.

There, around noon, Edward went to Cherry and called her from where she was playing with her other friends.

"Good afternoon, Your Highness!" Cherry bowed with gratitude.

"Good afternoon, love. I think ... you know why I summoned you," said Edward.

"Please do not send me to that witch! I mean to Doris. I can do anything for you but not this thing please. She hates me and stares at me as if she would kill me! I am sorry, but ..." Cherry made a long face, knowing why Edward was there.

"Why are you so afraid of her? She is just a sweet, beautiful, charming, and adorable young girl. And have you seen her hair?" Edward asked.

"Yeah, it is just like a bird's nest or a kind of mop—that is all. And adorable? I think you've made a mistake, and I am sure that you meant hateful. She is a terrible person." Cherry had started to hate Doris for obvious reasons.

"What do you mean?" Edward asked.

"Oh ... I am sorry, my prince. But you were telling what you think about her, so I also thought I'd tell you what exactly I feel about her," Cherry apologized.

"Okay, at least tell me where she would be at this time," Edward asked.

"She would be at Christine's bakery at this time," Cherry informed him.

"All right, then. Thank you, darling," Edward said with a smile.

"Oh, it is my pleasure, Prince Edward," Cherry replied.

Edward reached Christine's bakery after asking the people around for her address. Christine was doing some work at her table and didn't notice him.

"Hm ... excuse me, miss!" Edward said.

Christine raised her head and felt dazed and speechless upon seeing the prince at her shop. She stared at him and was not able to decide what to say. Feeling joyous, overwhelmed, and surprised made her stand still and just stare. For the first time in her life, he—the one she loved—was there, standing right in front of her. It was the first time he had ever spoken to her. But Edward wanted something or someone else. According to him, she was acting really strange.

"Hello!" He waved his hand in front of her eyes and continued, "Are you all right, miss?"

"What? I am absolutely fine. I mean, good afternoon, my prince. I am fine ... yes ... absolutely fine. I am sorry about yesterday," Christine said anxiously.

"Oh, was that you?" the prince asked.

"What? Oh, no. I mean it was not *me*." Christine realized the prince had not noticed her.

Edward's eyes were looking for Doris, but when he couldn't find her there, he tried to ask about Doris, hesitating, "Hm okay, do you work here alone? I mean ... are you alone here?"

Christine's eyes widened when she heard this from the prince. She interpreted it entirely differently, and what else could she think anyway? "Well ... yes, I am alone. I am sorry, I mean. I am working alone here. Anything you need, Your Highness?" she replied.

"Hm … sorry, miss. Wrong address," he said and ran from there, hearing and seeing Christine's weird behavior.

"Wait, sire. Please have this garlic bread here. It is new and quite delicious." Christine tried to stop him, but he didn't even look back.

Edward again went to Cherry and asked, "You told me that Doris would be there at Christine's bakery, but she said she worked there alone and there was no one else."

"Hm … Doris has always come along with Christine since the day she came here," Cherry tried to explain. "What did you ask, Christine?"

"I asked her … if she worked there alone," Edward answered.

"That is why you did not get an answer. That is not how you ask about someone! Anyway, since Doris is not there, I can go and ask about her there," Cherry said.

"All right, then. I shall wait for her reply here. Return soon." Edward was reluctant to go back there.

Cherry went to Christine to ask about Doris. But Christine was standing still outside, looking at a point continuously.

"Hey, Christine. What are you looking at?" But Christine didn't move even a bit.

"Hello! Where are you lost?" Cherry said, raising her voice.

"I'm ... what? Oh hi, Cherry. When did you come here?" Christine noticed Cherry.

"Just now. Where are you so lost?" Cherry asked.

"Oh, nowhere. I am so sorry, Cherry. I did not mean it. I ruined everything yesterday. I had made it with so much love for you. I feel so ashamed," Christine apologized for the cake.

"It is completely fine, Christine. It went well even after that. Why did you leave?" Cherry was a polite girl.

"How could I stay there after that? I was so embarrassed. I am even now." Christine was still sorry.

"Do not think that much. It happens. I am so much clumsier than you could ever be. And you had been working all day yesterday. You must be tired," Cherry said, understanding her.

"Oh, you are such an angel, Cherry. By the way, what made you come here?" Christine asked.

"Nothing, I could not help but wonder—Doris does not seem to be around here. Has she left this kingdom *forever*?" Cherry asked, hoping for the answer to be positive.

"Oh, no. She did not come today. She is at home. She felt tired after yesterday's work, so she did not come along. Why are you asking about her? Do you *miss* her?" Christine teased her, as she knew they both didn't like each other much.

"Hahaha! Nice joke. Who would miss her? I do not know why people admire her. She thinks the entire world revolves around her," Cherry wondered out loud.

"She is not that bad," Christine said.

"She is such a spoiled brat. She thinks she is a princess or something. Anyway, I can talk all day against her. But I have to hurry back. See you later. Bye." Cherry took leave of Christine.

"Hey, wait! Take this garlic bread. It is free for you and thank you for understanding me." Christine handed the garlic bread to Cherry.

"Oh! And you know, Doris gave me the idea for this one," Christine told Cherry.

"I already hate it then," Cherry said.

"Oh, it is not bad. Try it. At first, you might not like it, but it tastes good after. I guess, just like Doris." Christine winked at her.

"Gee, I am not sure about that. But since you have made it, I am sure it is good." Cherry left after saying that.

She returned to Edward and told him where Doris was. Learning of that, Edward didn't waste his time and went to her on his horse. Doris was sitting on a huge rock by the brook, facing the opposite side, and was throwing pebbles into the brook, with some of Christine's wild friends around her, grazing and doing their business.

Edward got off Maddox and moved slowly toward her with Maddox's rein in his hand.

"Hm ... Hey Doris, how are you?"

"Oh ... Hello, Joseph. I am good. You tell me ... how are you and your fiancée?"

Edward was surprised and tried to process the question, while Doris asked again, "Why did you not bring her yesterday to the celebration?" Doris said in a sarcastic tone.

"Fiancée?" Edward was confused but soon realized that he was Joseph to her, and Joseph was engaged. Someone must have told her about him. So, he tried to make something up. "Fiancée? Whose fiancée?"

"Don't try to be too smart, Joseph. I know that you're engaged. You're still hitting on me! You are ridiculous. I can't believe you." Doris was disappointed.

"No, you are getting me all wrong." Edward tried to make something up.

"No. I mean—yes, I was, but the engagement broke. She loved someone else." Edward blabbered whatever came to his mouth.

"Don't lie to me." Doris was aware.

"If I were lying, I would be wearing a ring. But I am not. Look," Edward said, showing her his hand.

"Old trick. You must have removed it before coming to me. I think it was you who started it, but I am not going to be the first one to be fooled by this stupid trick," Doris said, ignoring him.

"Oh, come on! Why would I lie about this? I swear that I am not engaged to anyone. Here, look at me. Do you really believe what you are accusing me of is true?" Edward asked Doris, holding her shoulders with both his hands and looking into her eyes.

Doris remained quiet, turned back, and started throwing pebbles into the brook again.

I Know the Story

"I am sorry," she said, looking at the brook.

"What? I mean, what for?" Edward had not expected Doris to apologize.

"For everything. I was such a jerk every time I met you even though you were so nice to me. You don't deserve my silliness and stubbornness." Doris was tired of her behavior, as nobody deserved it—at least not the ones she had met lately. It wasn't even fun bullying people without Kate and Cyril.

"Oh, that is completely fine. I think I have learned to be around you. And moreover, I feel I can handle you," Edward said. Doris remained quiet.

"Hmm, but if you must apologize, you could do something for me," Edward continued.

"And what would that be?" Doris asked.

"Dance with me here, will you?" Edward said, extending his hand toward Doris. It was just what he had heard from his parents. "Or maybe not," he said again, hesitating.

"LOL, that is *so* clever of you. You are taking advantage of me being sorry," Doris said, smiling.

Edward said nothing and smiled too.

"But there is no music," she said again, taking his hand.

"Who needs music? You can move to the music imagined by that beautiful mind of yours," Edward said.

Doris took Edward's hand and got off the rock on which she was sitting.

She put one of her hands on Edward's shoulder and held his hand with another, and they both started to move.

"Trust me, it's not as easy as you think. You haven't seen the true me yet," Doris said with a smile.

"What is?" Edward asked.

"Handling me," Doris replied.

Edward made her twirl and took her in one of his arms while still holding the other hand and said, looking into her eyes, "Is that so?"

"Woah." It really took Doris's breath away. His father's story was working. He was feeling wonderful to be that close to her. He felt the same way his father told him he had felt when he met his mother—he wished to dance with her for eternity.

"You looked breathtaking yesterday. I wanted to talk to you, but you left because of the accident," Edward said.

"Thank you. Christine felt tired after all the work she had done yesterday," Doris said, smiling.

"Oh. Is she fine now?" Edward asked.

"Yes. She went to work even after doing so much yesterday, and look at me: I did, like, nothing and feel tired even today," Doris said. Edward giggled.

"So, tell me about you." He wanted to know about her while they continued to dance.

"What do you want to know about me?" she asked.

"Like ...Who are you, where are you really from, who's your family and friends, and what do you like? I know nothing about you except for your name. And the last time I met you, you said you were lost." Edward knew nothing about her.

"Hm ... those are a lot of questions shot at once. Well, I happen to be lost here. That would be the shortest answer to where I am from. I have my mom, dad, and a little brother George in my family. I am closest to my dad. He is the coolest dad in the whole wide world. My mom and I don't really work. She is such a controller. Doris, do this, do that, don't do this and that—discipline, reputation, blah, blah, blah ... Ugh, she makes me accountable for everything wrong. I can't stand her sometimes. But I truly miss her so much now that I'm realizing how I have been. I feel it was my fault being so reckless all along, and she was just worried about me, which is only fair. Dad helps me every time I get into an argument with my mom. I bet she isn't missing me much. George is four years younger than I am. We are both like the biggest enemies," Doris said. But she didn't want to complicate it by telling him about the magic that had brought her there, so she kept it simple.

"Why? Your own brother?" Edward was surprised.

"Oh, no, no. You are taking me wrong. Not literally. We just fight all day. He is just so annoying. He spits out all my secrets to my parents when he finds them out, and he spies on me all the time to blackmail me to get what he wants. He thinks he is Sherlock Holmes," Doris told him about her brother.

"Sherlock who?" Edward asked.

"I would have not talked to you if you were in my time and didn't know Sherlock Holmes. But it's not your fault," Doris murmured.

"What?" Edward asked.

"Nothing. He is a famous fictional detective where I belong. He solves complicated mysterious crimes, I mean," Doris explained.

"Wow. Tell me more about you." Edward was curious.

"Hm ... I have two best friends, Katie and Cyril. We're real fun. I mean you wouldn't have liked me at all if I were in my original form. Well, I have been showing it but not much. They are both my childhood friends. We share, like, everything with each other. We are more like a clique and never add anyone to our group. I miss them. I wish I could tell them everything," Doris said, feeling excited at first and then low.

"Oh, so, what made you stay here if you miss them so much?" Edward asked.

"Let's just say I can't keep staying here. But I made a nice friend here, Christine. She is a wonderful soul. We have been sharing everything since we met. She has been so helpful to me. She taught me quite a lot of things. I trust her and tell her everything. Even she shares everything with me. LOL, she is *so* into the prince. We even had an argument over you and Prince Edward," Doris told him.

"I beg your pardon—what?" Edward didn't know that.

"She told me that you were engaged." Doris couldn't tell him that she had argued in favor of him over the prince (as far as she knew).

"Oh, I see …" Edward was also hiding the mix-up, so he didn't say much.

"I think Christine didn't know about the break-up then. She told me, so I thought she knew better about the people around here. Anyway, I'll tell her this," Doris said.

"Oh no, please do not tell her about this." Edward didn't want the wrong news about Joseph to spread.

"But why?" Doris asked.

"Oh, please no. You know how things spread, so please do not. It would be quite scandalous. It would bring shame to her family for eloping with her lover. And I do not want that." Edward said whatever first occurred to him.

"All right, I won't. You can count on me." Doris tried to be understanding.

"I count on you," Edward said with a lovely smile, moving both his hands around Doris's waist.

Doris felt nice as well. She had never danced like that with anybody before.

"So, what were you doing here alone?" he continued, to skip that awkward topic.

"Nothing," Doris replied.

"You looked lost in your thoughts when I came here. What were you so deeply thinking about, if it is not rude of me to ask?" Edward asked.

"Oh, not at all. I was just thinking about how life shows its different colors. For a moment, it's fantastic, and you're the owner of everything. But suddenly, it changes so much that you are left with nothing. And if you even get a glimmer of hope or happiness over something that you wanted your whole life, you are so scared of accepting that thing—because you fear that if you lose that thing, the pain will take you down. A person who always stays happy has to see struggles in their life as well… No one can live happily forever. Sometimes, life becomes so complicated that you get confused. You can't even understand whether you should be happy for whatever is going on or try to escape from there, fearing that it'll be taken away from you later and leave you in so much more pain. One has to face everything." Doris spoke to Edward in a soft manner for the first time and kept her head against Edward's chest.

"I am really surprised that a girl like you could be so deep," Edward said, wondering, but immediately regretted how it came out.

"What do you mean? Of course, everyone has emotions. Some people don't like to show it, but everyone has them." But Doris didn't feel offended this time.

"No, I thought you were a fun-loving and free-spirited girl. That is why I liked you. But now, I think I like you more," Edward said.

"You can't." Doris knew where it was going, so she stopped moving and got away.

"Yes, Doris, I can. I think I love you. You know that, and I am sure that you love me too as much as I do—do you not?" Edward spoke his heart out without hesitating anymore.

Doris looked at Edward, with her eyes full of pain and dilemma. Her eyes turned wet suddenly, as she wanted to pour her heart out but was not able to. She didn't want Edward to feel this much since she knew that she didn't belong there. She had the feeling that Edward loved her, but she didn't want him to say it.

"What happened, Doris? Tell me, do you not? I started liking you the first day we met. I do not know why I could not stop thinking about you. But I want to ask you, Doris." Edward got on his knees in front of her, held her hand, and continued, "Do you love me? Do you feel the same about me?"

Doris took her hands back. "Joseph, you know nothing about me. Why are you saying all these things to me? Please leave me. How can you love me without knowing me properly?"

"So what if you are not rich? So what if you are not a princess of any kingdom? You are my princess, and that is enough for me to know about you. And I do not need anything except you," Edward said.

"You do not understand me. Why don't you understand? Things are not limited to my economic conditions. And since we are talking about that, boy, you must know that my father is one of the richest in Florida. But leave that topic. The important thing is that something really strange is going on in my life, which I never dreamed of. I don't even know if this is real. I ... I ..."

Doris's voice got firm, and her whole body shivered perhaps due to nervousness.

"Hush … do not say anything, Doris. Just let me see that pain and love in your eyes … which just want to come out. You know, these beautiful eyes say a lot more than what you want to say," Edward said, standing and holding her hands.

Doris's was about to burst into tears as she felt emotional at the moment. The hard ice of her heart had melted. She felt stupid about it but couldn't stop it from happening.

"Doris, I know you feel the same about me. Maybe more than that. But I want to hear that from you. Just do not think about anything. Just say whether you love me or not."

"Joseph, you don't understand. It's not so easy to say—"

"That is not what I asked. If you want to say no, I will not bother you ever again," Edward interrupted.

"Hm." Doris was completely blank as she couldn't say anything, and she didn't know how to handle the situation.

"All right. I think it was just in my idiotic imagination that you loved me too as madly as I do. Sorry, Doris, for bothering you this much. But do not worry. I shall never ever come in front of you. And I apologize that you felt embarrassed because of me." Edward said, letting go of Doris's hands. "And goodbye." His voice cracked as he started going from there, having lost his hope.

"Oh God, these medieval people also had the tricks of emotional blackmailing. But why the hell do I care about it? Why don't I want him to leave? And why am I feeling like just crying in his arms? What the hell! I am not a stupid, emotional girl!" Doris murmured as she felt the flow of tears down her cheeks. Her hand moved to her cheeks to check them, and she found that she really was crying.

Edward was moving away from her with a heavy heart, holding Maddox's rein and with his eyes wet, but he expected that Doris would stop him. And sometimes expectations do work.

"Hey, Joseph," he heard Doris calling him, and in no time, he turned back, left Maddox, and came back toward her with triple the speed with which he walked away from her. "Hm ... yes?" he said with some hope.

"What the hell do you think of yourself?" Doris yelled at him. Edward now got a bit confused. "Where were you going without letting me say anything?" Doris shouted again.

"Well ... I thought ..." Edward was not able to answer that.

"Oh so, you think too," Doris teased him to lighten the mood.

"Excuse me!" Edward said.

"Can't you see that you said something that is a huge thing for a girl? She will have to take some time to decide, or she may hesitate to answer! But no, you just said whatever you wanted to and started leaving," Doris said.

"But I ..." Edward tried to speak.

"But what? I was thinking, all right? I just can't make out why I can't stop thinking about you all the time. I don't understand why I get so conscious whenever you come before me and speak or do some rubbish? Why do I remember each and every word that you say to me? Why do I see your idiotic face every time I close my eyes? I am not a shy kind of girl but …" Doris paused, as she said all these things in one breath in her loud pitch, which almost sounded like she screamed at him.

"But? But what?" Edward knew now what Doris wanted to say but tried to act innocent, as this was a thing that anyone would enjoy listening to.

"But I don't know why I'm feeling so timid to say it." She was still shouting, but now, her voice got softer as she continued to speak. "I think I love you too. I guess I really do," Doris said, looking right into his eyes.

Edward smiled. This made Doris a little shy and look down, but then, she again raised her head and said, "What? Yes, I admitted that I love you. Happy?"

"Doris." Edward had no words left to say after hearing what he wanted.

"Don't say anything now." Doris hugged him tight saying that.

The sun was about to set and had left a red light all around. The weather was extraordinary and had brought them both together. They were extremely glad and overwhelmed like never before.

And it was the happiest day of Doris's life.

Katie and Cyril who had been reading everything that was happening were really happy to know that she was fine, and there were people to look after her. Though Katie was worried, wondering what would happen if Doris found out Joseph was Edward, the prince with whom Christine was in love. They pretty much knew what happened in the story book but were not aware how the story would take shape with Doris in it.

Doris's parents were afraid that Doris was no more and were all gravely devastated. Her mother couldn't stand the pain, so she made up her mind to listen to Katie and Cyril, because they gave her the only hope that her daughter was alive, even though it was hard to believe them.

Chapter 13

Reality Hit

Doris was extremely happy. She had never felt this much happiness before. With all that love in her heart, which she could barely carry, she went running to Christine outside the door as soon as she returned. Doris was laughing, smiling, and blushing by herself. It was all like a dream. Yet, it was the time she wished would never end.

"Christine! Uh … I have so much to tell you. I love you. I love everybody here. It's so great in here," Doris screamed with joy.

"Oh my. You look so happy—the happiest I've ever seen you. What happened?" Christine was happy to see Doris happy.

Doris said nothing but just blushed.

"Doris is blushing! How is this even possible? I smell love." Christine took no time to read Doris's face. "By the way, I have something to tell you too. Looks like we both had a wonderful day," Christine continued.

Reality Hit

"Really? You go first because I am not going to stop if I start," Doris insisted while walking in with Crinstine.

"No, you were saying something, and I interrupted." Christine wanted to know about Doris.

"Say it, Christine. I don't want to fight again and then do the dishes alone at night." Doris wanted to take more time telling her story later.

"Okay, do you know Prince Edward came by to my bakery today? Oh, it was the first time I saw him up close. I am still not able to believe it." Christine was excited too.

"Hmm ... So, you are basically so excited because that prince of yours just visited you?" Doris said sarcastically.

"Oh, he spoke to me too." Christine tried to explain why she was happy.

"Oh, I see. The prince visited your bakery and spoke to you as well. Let me guess what his words were: 'How much do these muffins cost?'" Doris teased her.

"Doris, it would have been a big thing for me then too. But you know what he asked me?"

"Hmmm ... the price of cake?" Doris still teased her.

Christine stared at her.

"What? You said it wasn't muffins." Doris did not stop messing with her in her joyous self.

"He asked me whether I was alone." Christine said that as if it was a very great thing to be happy about.

"Did he? And what is that supposed to mean?" Doris tried to pull her leg. She knew that it was too much for Christine.

"Hmmm … I don't know. Maybe nothing." Christine hesitated but wondered.

"But what if it meant something." Doris reached Christine's ears from behind her and whispered. She didn't want Christine to lose hope. "What if he is interested in you?" she continued.

Christine didn't say anything but just blushed until her cheeks turned red.

"Awww … Look at my sweet sugar candy turning all red," Doris said.

"Oh, stop it, Doris. Maybe I am thinking more than I should. I mean I am nothing, but still, his visit to my bakery was the biggest wish I could ever have fulfilled. Anyway, we will see" Christine tried saving herself from more leg pulling. Even though she was happy, she didn't want to hurt herself by thinking it could ever happen.

After keeping her stuffs, she walked in the kitchen where she noticed that Doris had already cooked something. "Oh, what's this! You cooked!" Christine didn't expect that.

"What? I was extra happy, so I tried cooking… But don't get your hopes up, it's just porridge. And it might not taste that good." Doris said while eating a left-over muffin that Christine had brought from her bakery.

"I don't know what to say. You surprise me sometimes. Thank you." Christine was extremely glad.

"Oh, It's nothing. You worked all day and I had relaxed enough for the day, so I thought I could be of some use and give you a small break for tonight. Moreover, if you thank me for one meal, then I would have to thank you for about a hundred times. So, I guess we can just stop emphasizing this." Doris said while making Christine walk out of the kitchen holding her shoulder and pushing from her back and making her sit on the chair where they dined. Doris then served Christine on the table and served herself. "I guess I must ask about what you are so happy about. What happened today?" Christine enquired.

"Joseph. He said he loves me and made me accept that I do too. You know, suddenly, I realized that he is so dreamy. He took me in his arms, and we danced and looked into each other's eyes, and we both hugged. Oh, I really love him," Doris told her about what had happened.

"But Doris ... he is engaged. You know that, right?" Christine worried about her.

"Hm, yeah, about that. He isn't," Doris said.

"But he was. The whole town knows that." Christine was sure.

"Well, just say that that's a long story, and I know that he isn't now." Doris believed her presumed Joseph too.

"Really? This is just amazing then. I am glad that you are happy here after all. Just stay here. It would be great!" Christine said, reminding Doris that she was not in her own real world and woke her up from her dream.

"Oh my God, what do I do now?" Doris's expression changed suddenly.

"What?" Christine couldn't understand Doris's sudden change of expression.

"I mean I am in a book. So, he is a character in a book. There will be some day when I must leave sooner or later. Who knows what is actually going on? What if I someday marry him and this happens then? What would I do then? It is going to be so complicated. Oh! What the hell is happening?" Doris kept speaking of her insecurities.

"Doris, I think you are thinking too much. I somehow believed you then, but how can you say we are all some characters of a book? I am very much alive, and so is he. You must have some misunderstanding." It was hard for Christine to digest that she was just a fictional character.

"You wouldn't understand, Christine. I remember I was pulled by a book. Until now, it was all fine, but now, it is going too far. My life has become a play now. I can't decide anything." Doris began to worry.

"Oh, Doris, do not worry much. Every story has a happy ending. Even though you go through some bad phases, I am sure it all ends well." Christine tried to calm her down.

"That is the problem, Christy. It's not a story. It's happening in my real life." Doris started to panic.

"Everyone's real life is a fairy tale. Where do you think stories come from? It just depends on how well the narrators narrate the stories of their lives," Christine said.

"Where do you get these lines from?" Doris felt fine now.

"Ha ha! You know it comes naturally." Christine winked while getting up from the table after their dinner was over.

"I need to distance myself from him, Christine. You just don't understand what the circumstances might be. I was just immature to not realize that. I just couldn't see him sad and walk away like that. You know, he looked too adorable. I simply couldn't help but feel like comforting him and embracing him. It was like he enchanted me with his innocence. And now, look, a brief moment of weakness made me confess everything to him. I can handle myself, but I can't imagine hurting him if I am forced to leave as I was forced to enter," Doris said in the bed.

"I just wish for nothing bad to happen," Christine said.

"I hope so too." Doris sighed.

Christine slept peacefully after her long yet exciting day, but Doris couldn't. She could not help but think about all of it almost all night.

At the castle, Edward was in a similar state. He was delightful when he returned. Fitzgerald saw him and felt a sense of anger.

"Where have you been, my prince? We looked for you all day," Fitzgerald questioned him.

"Oh, Lord Fitzgerald, you must stop worrying about me all the time. I am too happy to answer that entirely now. Please make something up to Mother if she asks," Edward said to Fitzgerald and moved to his room joyfully.

"Oh, what is he so happy about?" Fitzgerald said to himself.

"Joseph? Joseph?" Fitzgerald called his son.

"Yes, Father?" Joseph came running to his father to find out what had happened.

"You are Edward's best friend. Ask him why he is smiling so much like an idiot." Fitzgerald wanted to know.

"Sure, Father," Joseph said and went to Edward.

"Hello, Edward. Where have you been all day?" Joseph asked Edward.

"Oh hello, my friend. You are just the person I wanted to see right now," Edward said with happiness.

"What happened?" Joseph asked eagerly.

"Do you remember that girl Doris—the one you saw at the garden the other day?" Edward asked.

"Er ... yes!" Joseph replied.

"Well, I love her so much, and she does too," Edward said.

"Oh, that is wonderful. I liked her that day." Joseph was happy for the prince too.

"I am glad that you liked her." Edward felt nice.

"But why were you telling her that you were me and I were you that day?" Joseph wanted to know.

"Oh, there was confusion in the beginning, but later, I just wanted her to love me as a person and not with the knowledge that I am a prince. Also, I didn't want her to know me through the impressions of other people. I wanted her to know me personally," Edward explained.

"So, are you not going to tell her?" Joseph asked.

"Of course. Now, I shall. I will tell her, and then, I will bring her to meet my parents," Edward informed. He continued telling Joseph everything about how it started, how he saved himself by cooking up a random story about Joseph's fiancée, and how his day had passed.

Personality Change

The next morning, when Christine and Doris were working at their bakery, Cherry arrived as if it were a routine she was lately made to follow.

"Good morning, Christine," she greeted, with full charm, and "Hey, Doris," she greeted with, hm, something completely opposite of charm.

"Hello Cherry, how are you? Do you want something?" Christine asked.

"Hm, yes, Doris." Cherry hated this.

"What do you want from me, you annoying tiny creature?" Doris asked threateningly as always.

"Edw—I mean Joseph wishes to see you. He asked me to send the message that he is waiting for you at the Royal Garden," Cherry told her.

Christine looked at Doris to see what she would do now.

Doris was happy and wanted to see him too, but she did not want this to go far. "Tell him that I have too much work today and I won't be able to come. Find another friend to play."

"But ..." Cherry was asked to bring a person with her by her prince, so she wanted to try harder—even though this person was Doris!

"But what? Did you not listen to me carefully? Go now." Doris was just being Doris to Cherry.

Cherry ran to Edward and passed him her message. Edward was surprised to get this message. He was not expecting this from Doris after all that happened just a day back. He began walking to go to Doris and ask her what the matter was. But he remembered that the girl with whom Doris worked would recognize him as the prince himself, and he did not want Doris to learn of this that way.

So, he turned to Cherry who was trying to sneak away as she knew he was planning to send her again.

"Cherry, are you running away?" Edward noticed her trying to sneak away.

"No, my prince. How could I? You were not saying anything, so I was just strolling back and forth. I was about to come forward too, but you just caught me moving backwards." Cherry did not want to look rude.

Edward sent Cherry with another message. She was very reluctant to go to Doris but couldn't refuse.

"Doris, Joseph has some important business with you. If you won't see him today, he won't see you ever." Cherry passed this message to Doris without a pause.

"What is it?" Doris wondered.

"Go and ask him yourself, you giant creature." Cherry was irritated to be stuck in this situation, so she said this to Doris and ran away as fast as she could.

"Wait … What? Did you see that, Christine? What did she just call me? How dare she? I am not sparing her this time," Doris said to Christine.

Christine just smiled and was mature enough not to say anything about their childish behavior. "Oh, spare that poor girl, and go meet him if you want to. Do not be so hard on yourself." Christine knew she wanted to go.

"Okay, just one time to see what's so important if you say so." Doris tried to pretend that she wouldn't have gone to him if Christine hadn't insisted.

Doris immediately went to Edward.

"Okay, Joey. What was so important?" Doris asked, approaching Edward and behaving in her same old way.

"So important? I wanted to see you. Did you really forget that we love each other?" Edward was a little surprised at Doris's question.

"Yes, I have. Don't you feel disgusted speaking of stuff like this? It was momentary affection. I'm not feeling the same now. And I think you must not too," Doris said, turning her back to Edward.

"I beg your pardon—what? Is this a joke to you? I see that you do whatever you love to, and I love that about you, but that does not mean that you hurt anybody's feelings." Edward was hurt and confused.

Doris started to walk away without saying a word.

"Doris ... wait. Did I do something wrong? Are you mad at me for something?" Edward held her hand, trying to understand what was suddenly wrong.

"Oh, Joseph ... don't do this." She gave him a side hug, keeping her head at his chest to console him.

Edward was too disappointed to speak a word. He started to leave when he saw Doris didn't have anything to say about it.

Doris felt bad too. Although she asked him to go away, watching him really leave with that long face was something she couldn't do.

"Joey ... wait," she finally said and held his hand as he did. She walked in front of him, placed her hand on his cheek, and said, "Joseph ... try to understand. Please don't take me wrong, but it's hard for me too. Things are not that easy here."

"Then, what is it? What is bothering you so much due to which, one day, you say you love me and, the other day, you ask me to forget everything? Do you have any idea how excited I was to see you today? I couldn't sleep the whole night because I could not stop imagining how meeting you today would be like. I just could not help myself but dream about you the whole time. And I thought you must be thinking the same. But now, I get it. You don't feel the same, and I will not force you to be with me." Edward was all broken. As a prince, there was hardly anything he couldn't get. He got whatever he wished for, and here, he could feel the pain of not being able to get what he really desired.

On the other side, Doris had also never heard anything like this from anybody before. She could feel the truthfulness and emotions in what Edward was saying. And after all, she had started to love him too, and seeing her man sad was disheartening for her as well. She just held his neck with both her hands and kissed him in the most passionate way she could, showing her love to him.

Tears rolled down Edward's cheeks, and he couldn't help but hold her closer by the waist with both hands. She kept her arms around his shoulder too.

"I love you, Joseph. I really do," she said. "It was the idea of losing you that scared me."

"What made you think that I was ever going to let you go? I don't know what scares you so much, but trust me, if anything ever sets us apart, I will come and find you." he whispered in response to her fear.

She hugged him with joy. It was the time she was feeling most secure.

"Hm, Doris ... may I ask you a small favor?" he said, still hugging her.

"Yes?"

"Don't call me Joey or Joseph," Edward said.

"Why?" Doris wondered.

"Hm, this is more like my formal name, and I don't like it much. My close ones call me Ellis." Edward asked of her this favor for obvious reasons. It was in fact his middle name. He had come to tell her the truth, but the moment was too good to be spoiled.

"That's strange. But if you don't like it, I shall call you Ellis from now on, Your Highness," Doris said.

"What!" Edward thought she knew for a while.

"What? Can I not call you that? You are my Prince Charming after all, even though you are not the real one. Why do you take everything so literally?" Doris said and hugged him again.

As it is said, if you really love somebody, you can't stay away from that person for long, and the same happened to Doris. She wanted not to think of the circumstances that could occur when she would have to leave. Nevertheless, as she could see that there was no way back home, she accepted the "then time" and started loving it there with Christine and Edward.

Doris found herself quite changed. She helped Christine daily, learned to be with her birds and other animal friends, met Edward whenever he called her with the help of Cherry, got along with Maddox, and practiced horse riding. But Cherry and Doris could not stand each other, even after the many days that had passed. Doris was just doing it for Edward, and Edward took her to different beautiful places to show her. He showed her all the beautiful sights of his kingdom. They spent most of their time at the end of the brook, where it ran down as a beautiful waterfall and was amazing like it was from some fantasy. Doris loved it all and, with time, learned to indulge herself there.

Their love life was going so well but with the lie that Edward was Joseph. Of this, Doris didn't have a clue.

A Tragedy

*H*ere, Edward was all in love with Doris, and there, Fitzgerald had some other evil plans.

He was successful in buying most of the men to his side.

One fine morning, Edward decided to finally arrange a meeting between Doris and his father. He approached the king's room with a lot of excitement but was traumatized when he opened the door.

The king was lying lifeless on the floor, with his neck brutally stabbed along with the baron Lord Cai stabbed in his stomach lying beside him.

Edward fell to the floor with sudden shock. A maid arrived behind him and screamed seeing the king dead. The queen arrived running on hearing the scream, followed by Fitzgerald and a few other people. The queen could not stop herself from crying out loudly falling on her knees. Edward held his mother with tears in his eyes and hugged her.

It was quite a dark day for them.

Arrangements were made for the memorial. The body of the king and the general were carried to the graveyard with honor.

Doris waited for Cherry to arrive, but she didn't. Confused, she had the idea to go to the castle and check for herself. When she entered, she couldn't believe her eyes. It was massive and better than the castles she had seen in movies. She started to wander. "This should have been the first thing he should have shown me," she said to herself. Soon, she realized that not many people were in there. She asked a maid and learned about the king's tragic demise. She had never met him, but the idea of how much it must have hurt Edward, who was still Joseph for her, made her run directly toward the abbey, where she found out the memorial was being held.

She noticed that he was standing beside the queen with tears in his eyes and was consoling her, who was crying without a pause.

Edward was surprised to see Doris there from a distance.

He needed her the most but had not expected her there. Doris stood there and waited patiently for him to get free. She could understand the situation and, while sitting, noticed the arrangements going on. She found it strange that Edward, who was Joseph for her, was consoling the queen and looked so miserable and broken while Joseph, who was Edward for her, worked and didn't look as sad as he should have been.

Joseph approached Doris while working when he noticed her. "Hello, Doris. Good to see you here. You did great coming here," Joseph said, innocently thinking she was the one who could help

A Tragedy

Edward heal his pain. But it looked suspicious to Doris to see the prince talk in a normal manner.

For the sake of formality, she said, "I am so sorry for your loss, my prince."

Joseph realized immediately that Edward had not told her the truth yet, so he had to act as if it were his father. "Oh, yes. I mean, thank you. He was a good man really. Uh, I must go check the arrangements," he said and sneaked away immediately. Doris smelled an evil intention.

Talking about evil, Lord Fitzgerald came and stood next to Doris.

"Hello, Doris," he said, with his usual heavy tone of voice.

"Oh hello, my lord. I'm so sorry about whatever happened." She bowed to Fitzgerald, feeling conscious that he was her lover's father.

"I stood by him all the time. It was only when he was murdered that I was not around." Lord Fitzgerald faked crying.

"Oh, I don't know what to say. I feel bad too, even though I never met him. I heard that he was a kind person and good to all. He didn't deserve this, but I'm sure he is in a better place now." Doris tried to console him.

"You don't know. I was thrown out by another kingdom on a false charge, but this man found me during the worst time of my life and made me his ealdorman." Lord Fitzgerald told Doris something that she never knew and to prove that he cared about him.

"Oh, how could anyone do this to such a great man?" Doris wondered.

"The prince ..." Lord Fitzgerald said and continued to fake cry, taking advantage of the prince's lie.

"What?" Doris was surprised.

He knew that she didn't know that the man she loved was the actual prince, so he showed Doris his own son and continued, "Why do you think the prince is not crying when his mother is not even able to compose herself? My son looks more devastated than him. Oh, the king raised him as his own son but couldn't raise his own son right."

"But people love the prince," Doris said.

"Why shouldn't they? They are all shown a lie. But I know the actual truth. I know how he actually is within the castle." Lord Fitzgerald was good at manipulating people. As he was trying so hard to make Doris believe whatever he wanted to, Doris believed him. Also, she had the impression that he was her lover's father.

Edward consoled his mother to an extent and came to Doris. Fitzgerald moved away, seeing the prince coming. Edward hugged Doris tight and started to cry, "You are the only person I want to see right now. Look at what has happened, Doris!"

"Oh, Ellis, I am so sorry. Don't cry, my baby. I love you so much. I heard he was more like a father to you and raised you like his own child and look how finely he has raised you. Please calm yourself." Doris felt bad too.

A Tragedy

"How can I? You did not see how brutally his neck was stabbed. I cannot stop thinking of that sight I witnessed this morning." Edward couldn't stop crying.

"I do get it. But who could do this? Isn't it surprising that amid so many people and security, someone killed the king within the castle and got away with it? This is not by some outsider but by somebody who could easily pass any security check." Doris spoke her mind.

"What do you mean?" Edward asked, wiping his tears.

"I mean someone from inside the castle has done it, and I'd put my money on the prince," Doris said.

"What rubbish!" Edward was the prince himself, and he could never think of doing it.

"I know it is hard to believe because he is your friend. But just think about it. Someone has murdered the king for sure. If there was some outsider, he could have called for a war or at least tried to take over the kingdom by now. So, the doubt goes to some insider. And just think what benefit it would serve anybody else more than the prince himself. He is next in line, and such occurrences were quite common back then." Doris told him whatever made sense to her.

"Doris, I want you to never say that. You do not know anything. You must not say this to anybody because it cannot happen and is not the truth," Edward said.

"Don't be so blind, Ellis. Look at him. He doesn't even look like he has lost his father just now." Doris showed him.

"That is enough, Doris. The heir apparent *is* next in line. He does not have to kill his own father. It is not like there are any other male heirs in line. Please leave me alone for God's sake." Edward shouted at her as he was not himself then and he did not have the energy to tell Doris that he was the prince himself.

"Fine! If you want to be so blind, then suit yourself. I am not saying anything, and I am out of it," Doris said in anger and ran away.

She knew that Edward was devastated but still felt bad that he didn't try to give any thought to what she was saying. Edward felt bad too that he shouted at her, but he knew she couldn't have understood that situation and Joseph wasn't sad enough because the king wasn't his own father.

On the way back, Doris saw people closing their shops and moving toward the funeral. The incident had made the kingdom mournful.

When she returned to the bakery, Christine was closing her shop too.

"Oh my God, Doris, where have you been? Did you hear the news? The king is no more," Christine said in a firm voice, running toward Doris.

"Yes, I'm coming from the funeral," Doris said with a long face.

"Oh, I was going to the funeral. Will you come?" Christine asked.

"No, I've been there. I think you should go. I will go home," Doris said.

"Okay, I will see you later." Christine took leave of her.

A Tragedy

Everyone was assembled to say a final goodbye to the king.

It was a gloomy day for all but a few. Everybody was mourning, but Christine noticed that Lord Fitzgerald was happy at the back when she passed him by. She heard him saying something that sounded like he was the one behind the incident. But she couldn't say that to anybody.

When Christine returned, she found that Doris had already prepared supper. Christine was a bit glad that Doris was helpful on such a long day. They both started to eat, and while they were at it, Doris tried to speak her mind.

"Aren't you worried or thinking about who might have done this?"

"Yes, I am. This was a murder and attempted by someone within the castle, without any doubt," Christine said in all seriousness.

"Exactly, at least someone is wise enough to be able to see that. I think the same, Christine. I had an argument with Ellis. He didn't believe me at all. I really think it was Prince Edward who has done this." Doris told her the same thing she had told Edward.

"What? Have you gone mad?" Christine was sad about the day.

"What? You said it was someone from the castle too. Who else could it be? Prince Edward is the only one who is going to benefit from the king's murder. What does *anybody else* have to do with it?" Doris said what was logical to her.

"Doris, I think we should not discuss anything further about this. Let us just not speak about it." Christine didn't want to get into an argument again.

"Christine, I get that you are so much into Edward. But you do not know his true face, and I saw it today. Edward didn't even look like he had lost his father today. He spoke to me as if everything was normal. You all can be fooled so easily, and he is just taking advantage of that. He must have put on his sad face when people gathered there. I saw him when not much people were around." Doris told her whatever she thought was right.

"That is it, Doris. First, do not bring this 'You are into the prince' into our conversations all the time to cover what you have to say, and the second thing is that it is Fitzgerald who has done this. I saw him and heard him say that he was happy that the first step of his plan was finally successfully executed. What else could he be talking about?" Christine told her about what she had seen and heard.

"What rubbish! Lord Fitzgerald was crying so much. He himself told me that he was helped by the king at his worst time. Why would he do that?" Doris wanted some logic there.

"Looks like you can be fooled more easily," Christine murmured.

"What? What did you mumble?" Doris heard her to an extent.

"I was saying that *I get you are in love with Joseph and Lord Fitzgerald is his father*, but this is the truth," Christine taunted her in the same way Doris always spoke.

"Christine, you are going too far now. Maybe he was talking about something else. And just give me my answer: Let's just assume that it *was* Lord Fitzgerald. How exactly would he benefit from this? Edward is next in line. He is the only one who would do it for the crown!" Doris was angry now.

A Tragedy

Both of them left their supper only half finished.

"I do not know. And about Edward, he is going to get the crown anyway. He did not have to kill his father for it. And besides, everyone knows how close he was to his father." Christine had her logic too.

"Oh, that's just another face he keeps showing you all. I was fooled too. I always thought he was a punk and couldn't do anything. But he appeared to be extremely clever and brutal, and Lord Fitzgerald is not getting any advantage here in any way." Doris couldn't help but make her point.

"Hmm ... unless he kills the prince too! Yes, this must be it. Oh my God! Fitzgerald will kill Prince Edward too and take over the throne. He must be planning a coup! Edward's life is in danger." Christine thought for a while, caught the exact thing that was planned by Fitzgerald, and panicked.

"Just hold your horses, Christine. You think twice before you say anything against Lord Fitzgerald. You are just blabbering whatever is coming to your mouth. How can you accuse Joseph's father of such a heinous act!" Doris had lost her cool.

"That is the problem, Doris. You are seeing him as Joseph's father. Not as Lord Fitzgerald. Try to think. If what I suspect is true, we must do something. You love Joseph. Just approach Edward somehow and warn him about this." Christine was afraid.

"Oh, that's enough madness, Christine. Just listen to yourself!" Doris was furious now.

"You do not listen to anybody." Christine was worried about the matter, apart from the argument.

"All right, then. Don't talk to me. Good night." Doris covered herself with her blanket.

There was silence all around in the castle, and nobody even had dinner. It was dark everywhere except in one room, and that was Fitzgerald's. He celebrated the death of the king by drinking wine and having nice food.

"I did it finally. After waiting for so long ... that stupid king—my mouth hurt smiling all the time around him more than doing some work. Now, I am so close to my ambition. Just that little *punk* is in my way and killing him will be a piece of cake. But I must do it before he marries that, Doris. Otherwise, I might have to kill one more. I will do it tomorrow and hold his memorial with the same arrangements. Oh, I am so clever, and then, the crown will be on my head. Oh, cheers to me." Fitzgerald was talking to himself and feeling happy on his own.

Christine's suspicions were so right. But who would listen to her?

The Conspiracy

The next morning, Fitzgerald was all set to kill the crown prince. He woke up early that day, as he did to kill the king, so nobody would see. He opened the door of the room and went closer to Edward's bed with light steps. When he pulled off his blanket, he found nothing, but pillows arranged to look like a person. He took no time to understand it was a decoy. He panicked and turned to find the prince and the queen at the door.

"Lord Fitzgerald, what are you doing here?" Edward was suspicious.

Fitzgerald was a clever person. He calmed himself and answered, "Oh, good morning, sire. I came here to check on you. I learned that you did not eat last night."

"So early in the morning?" Edward asked.

"Hm, yes, Your Majesty. I could not sleep all night. He was so close to me." Fitzgerald faked crying.

"Oh, Lord Fitzgerald, I know. I could not sleep at all too. I have been thinking about who might have killed him. Moreover, I was horrified by the macabre nature of the killing. Such hatred shown toward such good men! Lord Cai's family is also miserable," Edward's suspicions were quelled on hearing Fitzgerald's response.

"Time heals the pain, my boy. Do not think too much. Give your mind some rest." Fitzgerald spoke extra nicely to make sure the doubt, if any, could be dissipated, since he was caught there.

"I know, Lord Fitzgerald. However, I could not help but accept that what Doris said yesterday was partially right—that it was done by somebody within the castle." Edward had given some thought to what Doris had said even though he was upset then to accept it and think about it.

"My God, I cannot believe it. Who could it be?" Lord Fitzgerald asked, knowing everything and being the murderer himself.

"I do not know, but an enemy is surely living in the castle as one of our own people. I have asked our best men to look and be aware. Because whoever he is, he must be doing this for the throne, and that means the next one is me. And that is why I set this up, but you arrived here instead." Edward could never doubt the loyalty of his father figure, Fitzgerald, so he thought an outsider was living as their own staff in the castle.

"What has happened to our happy lives? First, my husband, and now, my son's life is in jeopardy. I cannot live if anything happens to you!" the queen cried, understanding the risk to her son's life.

"Oh Mother, do not worry. Nothing will ever happen to me. You must stay strong." Edward hugged his mom.

"Please do not cry, my queen. Your son's life is my responsibility. I will not let the enemy live any longer," Fitzgerald said.

"You are our only hope, Lord Fitzgerald. I am glad that Dafydd found you. And I am sure that you will not spare our enemy," the queen said.

"Yes, Your Majesty, I promise I shall not spare the enemy," Fitzgerald said.

There, Doris was upset at her place about the little argument she had with Edward after a long time. She just wanted to help.

Christine was also silent as even she and Doris had a little argument. She wanted to fix it, seeing Doris upset. "About yesterday, I am sorry. I know that you are in love with him. Yet, I spoke against Lord Fitzgerald. But trust me, I did not mean to. I just cannot think of Prince Edward's life being in danger. The mere thought of him in trouble makes me scared. I know that we can never be together, but I always pray for him to live long and happily. Nevertheless, I should not have accused Lord Fitzgerald. He has been here before I was born, I guess. The king sheltered him and made him the ealdorman. Nobody could be that evil to a person who gave them such a better life," Christine said to apologize.

"I am glad that you realized that. And it's completely okay. I am sorry too. Maybe I was wrong. No son would kill his father this way. He is anyway going to get the throne. It can't be him." Doris saw Christine's point too.

"Yes, he cannot. We all know him. He cannot do that. I know he is broken the most, and there is nobody who can see his pain.

He must be miserable within." Christine was worried about the prince.

"You really love the prince, don't you? And your love for him is so pure and epic. In my time, nobody is bothered about someone else that much. We do not stick to a person like this if that person doesn't want us, not for long at least. But you ... you inspire me. You give off a nice vibe and have taught me how to unconditionally love someone for real." Doris had changed there. She felt emotions and wasn't the same anymore. Love and friendship had taught her compassion to the core.

"I just want him to be happy, Doris. I do not expect him to even know me. He is just a dream for me. But the sweetest dream that I never want broken, even if that means I need to sleep forever." Christine knew the reality.

"I promise you, Christine, that I won't let your love story be a dream. I promise to make it possible and true. I will talk to Edward about it and make sure that he sees you and loves you. He would be so lucky to have you." Doris could see that Christine deserved what she desired.

"No, Doris. I would not risk turning him into a statue with my curse even if it could ever be possible. I cannot be with anyone in my life! I never even made friends in my childhood, except for one, but even she did not know about it because I never let her get close to me. How would I be able to marry a person? These gloves won't always work. I would want to touch him, hold him. Moreover, once he gets to know about my curse, he will definitely not stay with me." Christine spoke about her darkest fear.

"You had a friend too? I thought I was the first one. Why do I feel jealous? And why did you not tell her?" Doris said.

"Because I was afraid. Her name is Isabelle. She was very generous. Children teased me because I wore gloves all the time when I was little," Christine told Doris about herself.

"Oh, I wonder why," Doris said sarcastically.

"What?" Christine started to understand Doris's sarcasm.

"No, I mean go on," Doris said.

"She was the only one who felt bad for me and fought with them so that I would not feel hurt. She asked me about it several times, but I never told her the real reason. And she was so good to even understand it," Christine told her.

"What do you mean? Do I not understand?" Doris felt a little jealous.

"I never said that. You do. That is why I told you the truth without hiding it. I do not know why I could speak about it to you," Christine said.

"Hmmm ... Cool that I am the best person you could get. By the way, where is Isabelle now? You never told me about her before," Doris said.

"She got married a year ago and moved out with her husband. Everyone of my age is married except for me, and I do not think I could ever be." Christine realized this and felt low saying it.

"Aw, my sweet little princess, you will find one too. You know, you don't need a man to feel good. It is not always about finding a partner here. I don't understand the obsession with marriage in this era. But I get your loneliness here. And somehow, I happen to understand what we might feel at this age. I seriously wonder why it's happening to you." Doris felt sorry for her.

"I do not know. However, I always wonder who did this to me. I was just a child back then, and even now, I never think of doing anything wrong to anybody. What made a person curse me with this? Because of this, I do not let anyone come near me," Christine said with a long face, looking at her hands.

"There must be a loophole to this curse, and we will find that out. It happens in every fairy tale. In fact, one of the most famous loopholes happens to be the *true love's kiss*," Doris said, teasing her with a positive attitude and making her feel better.

"We will see." Christine smiled.

"Well, it sucked to have an argument with you," Doris said and hugged her.

A few days passed, and Edward didn't meet Doris. He was busy searching for the culprit and handling his mother and himself after the loss they had suffered. Fitzgerald tried to plot the murder of the prince with his men and made attempts on his life but failed each time.

Doris was upset with Edward but missed him, and since he did not call her, she helped Christine seriously at the bakery to distract herself.

One day, Edward called her to meet him at the royal garden through Cherry.

"How are you, Doris?" Edward asked in a low tone.

"Oh, so you remember my name?" Doris taunted.

"Of course, Doris. How could I forget you or your name?" Edward asked.

"Then, what kept you from meeting me for so long? No whereabouts, nothing. I know you were upset, but you said you loved me. How can you love me if you do not let me be part of your pain? How can you love me and not go crazy about meeting me? How can one resist the feeling of seeing his lover's face if he really loved her? You just forgot me," Doris complained.

"No, Doris, that is not so. I gave some thought to what you said. I am sorry I was rude to you the other day. However, I had too much work. We need to find the person who killed my fath—I mean, the king. Please do not talk like that, and try to understand me," Edward pleaded.

"I missed you so badly. Never do that to me ever again, or I will never talk to you," Doris said, with tears in her eyes. It was the first time she had expressed her emotions so openly to him.

"Oh, I missed you too, my love," Edward said, embracing her with a heavy heart, yet feeling the comfort of their love. "You are the only person I need right now," he continued, holding her tighter.

Fitzgerald saw both of them and went to them taking Joseph along to exploit the prince's lie for his own amusement. "Well, well, well. Look at these two lovebirds. I only admire your affection for each other." Fitzgerald interrupted them, which annoyed Edward a bit.

"What is it, Lord Fitzgerald?" Edward asked, irritated at being disturbed in the middle of a moment he was cherishing after a long time.

"Lord Fitzgerald? Why are you talking to your father like that? Are you mad at him or something?" Doris asked Edward, as she found it strange.

Edward immediately realized. But Fitzgerald tried to take over the conversation. "Oh, children are difficult to handle sometimes."

Doris smiled, thinking he was his father and keeping her head against Edward's chest.

"Bow before the new king at least, Son," Fitzgerald said to Edward, showing him Joseph.

Both Edward and Doris bowed with respect in front of Joseph, and that made Edward angry at Fitzgerald now. Joseph felt awkward, as he didn't want it. But Fitzgerald was finding it humorous.

"Now, what was it ... *Father*?" Edward asked, staring at Fitzgerald again.

"Oh, I forgot what I was here for! The queen is calling for you. She is not feeling well," Fitzgerald informed him.

"Oh my God, what happened to her?" Edward said, running toward the castle and leaving Doris.

Doris couldn't think of anything except for talking about Christine with Joseph, who she thought was the Edward still.

"I am sorry for your loss, Your Majesty. I hope everything gets better with time," Doris said to Joseph.

"Yeah, I wish the same," Joseph said with a sigh.

"Err, if you don't mind, may I suggest something to you? I mean I wanted to talk to you about something, Your Majesty," Doris asked Joseph, considering him the new king now.

"Hm, me?" Joseph was hesitant. He looked at his father as he was scared that he would ruin something.

"Yes. It might offend you, but I insist that you give it a thought. I stay with Christine. I suppose you are aware that I do not belong to this place and was lost here? She was the one who helped me and let me live with her. She works at a bakery, and she is as sweet as whatever she bakes. She is the most perfect girl you would ever find." Doris tried to speak about her friend.

"What?" Joseph was now more scared to respond.

"I know that if you look at her from the perspective of her social standing, she is a mere baker. But if you see her as a person, she is the best. She is a queen in fact. Trust me. And after all, you must spend your life with someone who can love you the most and make you a better person. She has changed a person like me, and I know she will keep you happy too because she loves you the most. Kindly give some thought to it, see Christine once, and give her a chance to win your heart. I know you are upset right now, and it is not the time to talk about things like this. But if you think practically, if someone loves you, it will help you go through this hard time. Hm, you may not think that it would help, but I'm confident it will be of the greatest help for sure," Doris said.

"Hm, okay. I will think about it." It was the only thing Joseph could think of saying to avoid any trouble for Edward.

Fitzgerald understood everything and said, "You are such a nice girl, and your friend must be like you too."

Doris was very happy to hear this, and she left to tell Christine everything.

Fitzgerald was thinking of engaging in yet another foul play now. *She loves the prince, but she doesn't know that he is the prince, and her friend loves the prince too. What if I tell her dear friend that Doris is seeing Edward behind her back and deceiving her? It will trouble Doris, and trouble for Doris means trouble for Edward. Oh, it will be fun seeing the girl leave him before he dies. Oh boy, that is a jackpot*, he thought.

Doris reached Christine's bakery with excitement.

"Christine, guess what?" Doris asked, breathing heavily as she had come running to her with joy.

"Slow down. What is it? You look so happy after days," Christine asked with a smile, excited to know what had made Doris so happy.

"When you hear me out, you will cry in joy too," Doris said, taking Christine's hands and dancing.

"Will you please tell me now? I cannot think of anything that may make me dance with joy." Christine was curious to know too.

"I spoke to Edward about you," Doris finally told her.

"Oh my God! This cannot be true. You must be joking." Christine couldn't believe it, but bliss immediately consumed her.

"Why would I joke about it? It is true," Doris said, smiling.

"What did he say then? I know he would not have said yes for sure. Was he angry though?" Christine asked.

"No. Had he been angry, I wouldn't be dancing over here with you," Doris said.

"So, what did he say?" Christine could feel butterflies in her stomach.

"Hm, he said he would think about it. But just imagine that he sees you, falls in love with you, and says yes." Doris started to daydream and also made Christine imagine it.

"Oh, you are the most insane person I know," Christine said, blushing.

"Am I not?" Doris winked.

Christine didn't say anything but was unable to hold her happiness. She didn't care about the result but was happy that Doris took a step for her, which was the biggest thing she could have asked from anybody.

"Oh, don't think too much. He will definitely say yes to you. My heart says he would love you the most because you are adorable," Doris said.

"What makes you think that?" Christine asked, laughing at Doris's innocent, positive attitude.

"Well, why wouldn't he? You are the best person. You can handle anything and anyone with grace and sweetness. You are like a princess in some fairy tale who deserves a Prince Charming and gets one at last too," Doris said with all the love she had for Christine.

"I do not know and do not care about whatever happens next, but what you have done for me is like my only wish that you granted. How will I ever be able to repay you for this?" Christine was overwhelmed.

"Oh, you are just being silly now. You have done much more for me than anybody could have done. I was a mere stranger. I was so bad to you, and yet, you helped me and are still helping me. Moreover, you even handled my mood swings. If I were a guy or not straight, I would definitely date you. That was the least I could do for you," Doris said.

Both of them were very happy, and their friendship was at its peak.

When Edward reached his mother's room, he found her sick.

"Oh Mother, what happened?" Edward asked.

"Oh, nothing, my son. I just do not feel so good," the queen answered.

"She has not been eating properly and hence got unconscious, so I called for the physician." Edward's maternal aunt had been staying with her sister since the demise of the king.

"Is she going to be fine?" Edward asked, looking at the physician.

"Yes, Your Majesty. It is just that she is weak because she is not eating properly. Also, she is depressed because of her loss. I understand that it is not possible to cheer her up, but at least try to keep her happy, and do not let her think too much. Try diverting her mind to something else. She can get better, but if she remains the same, it could also get worse. There is nothing I can do apart from this. She has to eat, remain strong and be a little happy," the physician said and took leave of them.

"Oh Mother, do not do this to me. Am I nothing to you?" Edward couldn't see his mother like that.

"Do not speak like that. You are the most precious thing to me, my son. It is just that I never knew how to live without your father. You know, a princess is always taught to control her emotions and be strong, as she may be a queen someday and face the misfortune of losing her husband in battles or something else. I was taught the same. But I miss him, son. And I am miserable. I am not handling it well," the queen mother said with tears in her eyes.

"I miss him too, Mother, but you cannot fall ill. We only have each other. And you need to live for me if I am so precious to you. I know that Father is not here with us, and that thought kills me. But do not ever feel lonely. I am here with you all the time. Aunt Eira is here for you. Why do you feel lonely? Again, I know Father is not with us, but we are here. You may tell me anything you need anytime," Edward said to his mother and was worried about her.

"Yes, Sister. You cannot live like this, and I cannot see you like this. I should have taken more care of you." Eira was concerned about her younger sister.

"No, Eira. You have already done a lot. You have left your children and husband there for so long just for me! I feel really bad for all that you have done for us," Ffion said.

"Oh, nonsense! You are my baby sister. Of course, I will be here wherever you would need me the most. And you know how much I like being with you. Because you were so full of life, I do not like this version of you. However, fear not. I am here," Eira said to Ffion. "There is one thing we need to do, Edward," Eira continued to say to Edward.

"Anything, Aunt Eira." Edward knew only Aunt Eira could cheer his mother the most at this time.

"We need to arrange a coronation ceremony for you." Eira spoke about the coronation.

"What? So soon?" Edward was not ready.

"Yes, why not? It has to be done sooner or later, so why not soon? What do you say, Sister?" Eira asked.

"Well, Dafydd and I had planned that we would do it after Edward got married, so his wife would also get to see the coronation and be the queen. But it looks like we need to do his coronation first anyway," the former queen said.

"But, Mother, is this the right time for it?" Edward asked because he knew that the people and he himself were not over the king's demise.

"It is the right time, Edward. I know this might appear too soon to many because we are all still mourning. But I say Dafydd would not want to see you like this. He loved you so much that seeing you like this would kill his soul. It is indeed affecting your health. A coronation is the best thing you can do now. It is important and will help keep people busy and divert their minds to a big extent," Eira suggested.

"I think your aunt is right, Edward. It is the right time. It would have been nicer if your father were here, but since that is not possible, we need to give people their king. The throne should not be kept empty for long." The queen asked Edward to take over the throne.

"All right, Mother, if you say so." Edward also agreed, as it could help keep his mother distracted and happy.

"Where is Fitzgerald? We need to ask him to make arrangements." Eira asked for Fitzgerald. She enjoyed giving him work, as she never liked him much.

"Yes, I will talk to him, Aunt," Edward said while feeding his mother and tucking her into her blanket to comfort her.

When Fitzgerald came in, Edward was furious at him.

"I need to talk to you, Lord Fitzgerald," Edward said in a firm tone.

"Yes, sire, what is it?" Fitzgerald asked, knowing that he was mad at him because of his behavior in front of Doris.

"Please do not act like you do not know anything. Why did you do that in front of Doris?" Edward asked in anger, as he had been going through so many things lately.

"I came to tell you that the queen was asking for you, and when I saw Doris with you, I tried to help you with your lie, so it wouldn't make her suspicious." Fitzgerald was angry too when Edward talked to him like that for the first time, but he calmed himself and gave him an explanation.

"First of all, it wasn't a lie. It is what she assumed from the beginning. I just never corrected her, as I wanted her to know me and love me as a person and not bow every time in front of me because I happen to be a prince. And second, I never asked you to help me with this. I am going to surprise her at my coronation anyway," Edward said.

"Your coronation?" This shocked Fitzgerald to his core. He knew that Edward was next in line and that it would happen. But he was planning to kill him before it did. Listening to him made him furious.

"Yes, Mother wanted to talk to you about this. She is resting for now. Please see her only after she wakes up," Edward told Fitzgerald.

"Of course, Your Majesty, I will," Fitzgerald said in a firm voice.

"I am sorry about how I spoke to you a moment ago. You are like my father, and I shouldn't have spoken to you like that. I don't know why I got agitated so easily. I've lately had so many things going on in my life, which is more than I can handle." Edward apologized when he realized Fitzgerald looked lost.

"Don't worry. I will help you and take your entire burden," Fitzgerald said and left.

Later, he met the queen mother to discuss for the same arrangements. The queen mother asked him to arrange the ceremony within a week and invite all the kings and queens from other kingdoms who were their allies and every citizen to attend the feast following the ceremony.

Fitzgerald tried to calm himself down for the time being, but when he was finally free after a long day, he couldn't hold it any longer. He went to his room and broke everything up in anger.

"I did not wait for so long to see this Edward grow up to become the king. I didn't kill the king so he would get the throne. Oh, I have waited so long, and now, I won't wait any longer. The throne is mine. I will kill him on the same day of his coronation. Everyone will be there, and every arrangement will be made but only for *my* coronation," Fitzgerald said to himself and laughed.

The Surprise

The preparations began at the castle. Everyone got busy with their work. Edward wanted to inform Doris about this first, so he called her.

"I have news for you," he said to Doris.

"News?" Doris asked.

"Yes, but before that, I need you to close your eyes first," Edward said.

"Oh, so you have a surprise for me?" Doris was excited.

"Hm … yes, but how do you know?" Edward was confused.

"You obviously ask one to close their eyes only when you have a surprise. Hm, that was a spoiler, wasn't it? Gosh, why do I speak so much?" Doris knew that there was a surprise, but she also realized that she should have simply closed her eyes when she was asked without spoiling it. Edward held her waist and kissed her when she kept talking.

The Surprise

"Close your eyes," he whispered romantically.

Doris just smiled and closed them.

"I just want to speak my heart out to you," Edward whispered into her ear.

Doris's smile grew bigger, as his words tickled her from within.

"I've had everything in life since I was born. It was like the whole world revolved around me—a nice place to live in and the most wonderful people as my parents, who have provided whatever I have asked for. But still, there was something missing in it. And that was you. I never realized it until I met you. You are so much fun, the most romantic person I could ever imagine, and the most gorgeous woman I have ever seen, with equally gorgeous hair over which I swoon all the time. And most of all, you are the one who loves me more than anyone could ever love me with all your heart. I love you, Doris, and I love your uniqueness, which is sour but sweet from within. You keep saying that I don't know anything about you, but trust me, I am the one who knows you the most, even more than you know yourself. And I would be the luckiest man if I could spend the rest of my life with you."

Doris understood what Edward was going to say. She knew that there was a surprise, but she didn't expect that. She couldn't hold herself from opening her eyes anymore, and when she did, she saw Edward on his knees with a very beautiful and an expensive-looking ring she had ever seen in an equally beautiful box in his hands.

"Oh my God." She couldn't believe that she deserved so much in her life. She just closed her mouth with both her hands and fell to her knees with gladness too. Her eyes suddenly filled with tears of joy, and her heartbeat began to rise. She had never imagined she would experience this kind of a moment. She was the happiest in her life, and it surprised her that she could ever get this emotional at the same time.

"Will you honor me by considering my hand in marriage?" Edward said those beautiful words that could make any girl go crazy for a moment.

Doris immediately hugged him with utmost glee and said, "No. I will not."

"What?" Edward asked.

"Oh, you are such a teddy bear to handle. Of course, I will."

"I have one more thing for you," Edward said.

"What?" Doris said with excitement.

Edward presented her with a big box with a delicate and ethereal dress in it.

"Oh my God! Is that for me?" Doris asked.

"No, it's for your friend Christine," Edward said sarcastically, the same way Doris was in the habit of speaking.

Doris hit him on his arm for saying that. "I love this. Oh, this is the best day of my life."

"I have a news for you too," Edward said again.

"Oh, this is too much to handle in a day. What is it?" Doris asked.

The Surprise

"Prince Edward is going to become the king next week. I want you to wear this for the occasion. I want to introduce you to the queen, so I want you to look the best."

"Oh, that is so great. Even Christine would be happy listening to that," Doris said.

"There will be one more surprise for you that day." Edward decided to tell her about him being the prince that very day.

Doris was out of all options to guess what else he could surprise her with.

"What can it be?" She tried to think.

"How will it be a surprise if I tell you now? Anyway, I am going to be really busy, so I won't be able to meet you for long. Is that fine by my lady?" Edward asked.

"I can handle that. But keep meeting me even if not for long. I can't stay away from you any longer," Doris said with love.

"Of course, my love. I can't stay away from you either," Edward said, hugging her, and took leave of her.

As always, Doris told Christine everything in detail, and Christine was so happy for them upon hearing about the prince's coronation.

"Oh, I love this place now, and I don't want to ever go away from here. I wish it could include my parents and friends too. I wish there was something that could mix both of my lives. I just don't want to lose any of it. I miss them all so much today—Mom, Dad, George, Kate, Cyril, all of them. This is so big, Christine. I am going to get married to the love of my life. Whatever is happening is the greatest joy of my life, and I want them all to be part of it and share my happiness. My mom would be so happy to see me like this. She always complained that I won't be able to settle with someone with 'that' attitude toward everyone. I want her to see how Ellis is and how much better he makes me. I want her to see how responsible I have become now, as she always wanted me to be. I miss my dad, and I want him to walk me down the aisle and give me away. I want to apologize to George for having been a terrible sister. I want to tell Kate and Cyril everything. I know they will be happy to hear about all of this. I want all of them to meet you. I do not understand what has happened to me, but it is truly wonderful. And it would be the best if they were here too." Doris missed her close ones too much for the moment.

"I understand that you miss your family. Getting married is the biggest thing in a girl's life. It introduces you to your emotional self. It is the start of a new life in a new place all over again. I hope you get to see your family and friends when you get married. Until then, I am here for you to be your bridesmaid. I was the bridesmaid at Isabelle's marriage too. Now, it's time to be a bridesmaid again. You will go too," Christine said, consoling Doris. She was happy for her but felt a little sad that she will be alone again.

"Oh, my sugar candy, I am not going anywhere from this kingdom. And trust me, I am not leaving you alone. I promise that I will only get married if Edward accepts you or at least gives you a chance and gets to know you. Until then, I am here to bother you like always," Doris said, knowing that Christine felt upset about her being left alone again.

"That is not possible, Doris. I am really happy for you. Please don't spoil it for me. Be practical. I can't be with anyone, and King Edward would never fall in love with a girl who sells muffins in his own kingdom. Also, my curse …" Christine knew about her reality, and she didn't want to daydream anymore.

"Oh please, don't start with that 'my curse, my curse' again. A promise is a promise. And I will make sure it happens. I will make sure that you get a happy ending," Doris said, assuring her.

They went on talking, and Doris showed Christine the ring and dress that Edward had given her. Then, Christine showed Doris the dress she had made for herself, for "the day" that might come.

She Is a Witch

The news spread to the entire kingdom like wildfire. People were very happy and started to decorate the kingdom for their new king. Days passed quickly.

Only two days remained for the event. Doris went to meet Edward, as usual, along with Cherry.

Fitzgerald was asked to personally invite all the people of the kingdom, so he did his job along with his son Joseph. They reached Christine's bakery, and seeing Christine reminded Fitzgerald to cause trouble in paradise.

"Good morning, Lord Fitzgerald. Good morning, Sir Joseph. How are you both?" Christine bowed courteously.

"We are all fine. We have come to invite you to the coronation ceremony of his Majesty, Edward, which is the day after tomorrow. Everyone in your family can attend the event and the feast following it," Joseph invited her politely.

"Do you work here alone? The queen has asked us to invite everybody," Fitzgerald asked Christine on purpose.

Joseph couldn't recognize Christine properly, as he had never met her but had just seen her at Cherry's birthday celebration. Christine found it strange that Lord Fitzgerald was asking such a question, though he knew Doris. Doris had, in fact, told Christine that Lord Fitzgerald had talked to her and knew her.

"Hm, yes, my lord. I am Christine, a friend of Doris." She still tried to remind them, as she thought they perhaps didn't know her by face.

"Doris? Oh, yes. So, you are Christine," Lord Fitzgerald said, and Joseph also recognized her.

"Yes, that is me." Christine smiled, seeing that they recognized her. "Sir Joseph, where is she now? She went to meet you with Cherry," she continued, looking around for Doris.

"Doris to meet my son Joseph? Why would she come to meet him?" Fitzgerald chuckled.

"Hm, Father, I think we should get going now." Joseph sensed that this might cause trouble, so he tried to make his father leave.

"I am sorry to question you, sir, but seriously, where is Doris? Have you two fought? Because she hasn't returned after she went to meet you," Christine asked, looking at Joseph.

"No, miss. It is not so. She is ... she is ..." Joseph tried to think of an answer.

"She is with his Majesty." Fitzgerald spoke before Joseph could think of anything.

"What?" Christine was surprised.

"Father ..." Joseph tried to stop him. "I mean she had something important to discuss with the king, so she went to meet him while I got busy with my work," Joseph said, trying to handle the situation.

"Oh, I see. Maybe she went to talk about me," Christine, being a positive thinker, smiled and mumbled.

"No. She goes to meet him daily. They are getting married. Why would she meet Joseph? Joseph is already engaged. What is going on here?" Lord Fitzgerald heard Christine and said it all straight, trying to show that he was unaware of the situation.

"King Edward and Doris? What are you saying?" Christine couldn't believe it.

"Father, let us go. We need to invite so many people." Joseph couldn't think of anything else after everything was now laid open. He felt angry at his father.

"But this poor girl needs to know the truth if her friend has not told her yet," Fitzgerald said to his son.

Christine stood silently in disbelief.

"Oh, my sweet little child, Doris meets Edward daily, and they are both head over heels in love with each other and are getting married. His majesty plans to introduce her to his mother and announce their marriage on the same day. Although that last part is a secret kept from Doris, everything else is well-known by everyone in the kingdom. He sends Cherry to call her. I thought she has told you since you claim she lives with you." Fitzgerald told her the entire story while taking a muffin from the shelf and eating it. "Oh, this is delicious by the way. We shall place orders for gingerbreads and muffins here," he continued.

"No, that is not possible!" Christine cried.

"I am sorry, miss. I heard that you like Edward too. She once told me about you. I couldn't recognize you at first. Please don't tell this to Doris as she doesn't kno—" Joseph tried to explain.

But Fitzgerald interrupted, "Oh, I thought you would be happy for your friend. She is still with Edward. Do you want to see them with your own eyes?"

"Father, will you please stop this!" Joseph said to his father in anger.

"What? Did I say something wrong?" Fitzgerald said, acting innocent. But Joseph knew how his father was.

"Yes. Could you please take me to them? I want to see this with my own eyes," Christine said, wiping her eyes.

"No, we do not have time for this. We really are busy," Joseph said, avoiding the task of taking her there.

"Oh, don't be so rude, Joseph. You go and do the job of inviting people, and I will take this innocent girl there to them," Fitzgerald said, looking at Joseph. Joseph stared at his father, but Fitzgerald ignored him and continued, "I will join you after this."

Joseph left the place, as he couldn't think of handling it in any other possible way. Also, he needed to do his job.

Fitzgerald took Christine with him to the place where Edward and Doris met regularly. On the way, Christine was still hoping it was all wrong and just a deception by Fitzgerald. But when they reached there, she saw them together, kissing.

"No ... Oh God, please no!" Christine cried.

"Oh, I was not supposed to watch this. It's a crime, but I needed to help you. Let's go from here. It would not be good for me if his Majesty sees me," Fitzgerald said to her and took her back.

Christine didn't say anything on the way. But Fitzgerald fueled the fire. "I think she has betrayed you. How long have you known her? I can't imagine people are like this. She just used you for her benefit by not telling you the truth."

Christine's dreams were shattered, and she was devastated. She just reached her bakery, took her belongings, closed it, and left for her house, trying to hold back her tears outside.

When she reached home, she burst into tears. She looked at the dress Edward had gifted Doris and cried her eyes out. "Why did you do this, Doris? I knew that Edward wasn't for me, and I never even imagined I could be with him. But you deceived me, Doris. I would have understood it, had you told me directly that you loved Edward. I do not own him. But why did you manipulate me in this situation so much? How could you do this to me, Doris?"

On the other side, Doris eagerly tried to ask what the surprise was that Edward planned to give her on the day of the coronation. She couldn't guess what it might be.

"Oh, come on, Ellis. Please tell me what it is. Christine and I keep guessing what it could be like idiots all the time," Doris asked Edward.

"Christine too?" Edward asked.

"Oh, she is my best friend over here. We share everything. She is so happy for me too and is going to be my maid of honor on our big day."

"Nice. Joseph is going to be my best man," Edward said.

"What?" Doris asked.

"Oh, I mean Edward is going to be my best man. Did I take my own name for the best man?" Edward laughed to pretend he felt silly.

"He will?" Doris asked.

"Why wouldn't he? He has been my only mate since childhood," Edward said.

"But he is a prince, I mean a king now." Doris doubted if this was true.

"What does that have to do with friendship?" Edward asked.

"I feel stupid that I thought that he was a punk then," Doris said.

"You thought so?" Edward asked, laughing.

"Yes." Doris giggled. "Anyway, it will be so cool. We will let them both dance, and then, they will talk. Eventually, Edward will fall for Christine's beauty. And they will end up together. This is going as smoothly as I had planned."

"What are you talking about?" Edward couldn't understand.

"I mean Christine is *so* into Edward. And she is such a wonderful person. She is so beautiful by looks as well as soul—basically, an all-in-one package. Only a fool wouldn't fall in love with her. She loves him with all her heart, and nobody can love him more than she does," Doris told Edward about Christine.

"Doris, you need to stop making plans like that," Edward said, realizing this can cause trouble later.

"But why? I promised her that I will only marry you when I get Edward to meet her and fall in love with her," Doris said.

"How can you promise someone that?" Edward felt this was wrong.

"What do you mean? My friend loves him, and I just promised that I would help her. What is so wrong about that?" Doris asked.

"I mean, how can you promise her without knowing what Edward wants? You cannot choose a person for him without his will," Edward said.

"Wait, I have not chosen a person for him. She loves him so much, and I just said that I will make sure that it works out. There is a difference. I know it will be up to him, and I am not going to force him to like Christine. What is wrong in trying? And I am sure that he will like her," Doris said.

"There is nothing wrong in trying but to assume that Edward would love her …" Edward felt weird.

"Why? Because he is a king?" Doris asked in anger.

"Stop bringing the 'He is a king' argument into everything. Think of him as a mere person. Would it be right to promise your friend to someone? What if he loves someone else?" Edward tried to make her stop thinking about Christine and himself.

"You know what … Just leave it. You do not understand anything. I thought you would help, but no. And you really assume I would just blindly loose an arrow like this? I spoke to Edward about her, and he said he would think about it," Doris said.

"You talked to him?" Edward asked.

"Yeah, huh," Doris replied.

"God … why don't you understand? Just stop thinking about this. I need to go now. Take care. And I won't be able to meet you tomorrow. I have guests to attend to. Please do come to the event. I will be waiting," Edward said and left.

Doris felt bad that Edward did not support her, but she still moved to the bakery with the intention of proving him wrong by making everything work. But she was surprised to see that Christine wasn't there. Christine had never left without Doris before. But since it was dusk, she went home looking for her.

When Doris reached Christine's cottage, she found the door open.

"Hey, Christy, why did you leave without me?" Doris said, entering the cottage and felt shocked when she found everything broken and shattered around.

"Who did this? What happened here, Christine?" Doris was scared looking at everything around and finding Christine sitting on the ground in a corner.

Christine was sitting, hiding her face in her knees and arms, and said nothing.

"Christine, you are scaring me. Will you please tell me? Who did this?" Doris asked again.

"You did this to me, Doris. You did this. Why did you deceive me? I trusted you so much and loved you more than a sister," Christine said in a low tone.

"What are you trying to say, Christine? Will you please be more precise?" Doris couldn't understand anything.

"Edward. You know that I love Edward. Then, why did you do this?" Christine spoke loudly.

"What? What did I do?" Doris asked.

"Oh please, Doris. I don't want to talk to you at all. I seriously do not have the energy to say anything." Christine was devastated.

"I seriously do not understand—"

"Christine, Doris, what is happening?" It was Cherry's grandmother.

"Oh, your timing," Doris mumbled and turned to find Adyren just like she thought. "Nothing, Aunt. What is it?" Doris asked with a smile trying to be polite.

"What has happened here? Why is everything broken? Did anyone rob this place?" Adyren showed concern.

"No, nothing like that so far, but I was trying to figure that out myself," Doris answered.

"What happened, Aunty? You do not look fine," Christine asked, standing and wiping her face.

"Oh, have you two seen Cherry? She has not returned home yet. When I last saw her, she said she was going to call Doris. I was wondering if she came here." Adyren enquired.

"She must be playing somewhere with her friends. Anyway, kids at this age are really annoying and become such a troublemaker sometimes," Doris said.

"No, she always returns from wherever she goes, as she is afraid of the dark." Adyren said.

"Not everyone is like you, Doris," Christine spoke, looking at Doris. "Did you ask her friends?" She turned to Cherry's grandmother.

"Why are you talking like that? What did I do now?" Doris asked.

"You said you saw her last with Doris, right? Maybe she knows," Christine said to Aunt Adyren, ignoring Doris.

"No. I don't know. She came to call me and then went to play like always. Don't suspect me of losing her." Doris didn't know anything.

"Oh, my little girl, where might she be? I sense she is in some trouble." Adyren was really worried that she did not find her with Doris.

"Oh, please do not worry. We can look for her with you," Doris said, seeing her worried.

Christine said nothing. She felt too broken to do anything but couldn't say no either, as it was Cherry, and her aunt always took care of her as a godmother after her mother was gone. They started to search for her around, and it was getting darker. Adyren started to worry more as negative thoughts started to get to her.

"Oh, my little child, I hope you are fine," Adyren prayed.

"It's getting dark, Aunt, and I think we must look in your house once again. She may have returned," Doris suggested.

"She doesn't want to help, Aunt. She doesn't care about anybody but herself. Let her go. We will look for Cherry on our own," Christine said to Cherry's grandmother, as Doris was someone she didn't want to be with at the moment.

"What is wrong with you? Why the hell are you talking like that?" Doris wanted to know what the matter was.

"If you both do not wish to help, I can look for her on my own. But please don't fight like this. I am already very worried," Adyren requested.

"Sorry, Aunt," Doris and Christine said together and then stared at each other.

When they went to Cherry's house, she still wasn't there. Her parents had been looking around too and were hoping she was with Christine and Doris. But seeing them without her now concerned them more.

"Where might she be? My little girl," Cherry's mother cried.

"She will be all right, Martha," said Christine to Cherry's mother.

"I just hope so. But she hasn't returned yet, and it's so late," Martha said.

"I think we must inform the king about this. He might help us search for her," Doris suggested, seeing that they were unsuccessful in looking for her.

"But it's his coronation day after tomorrow. He must be busy with that. Most of the royal guests have arrived at the castle too. Would he help us out in this matter?" Cherry's father asked.

"Why wouldn't he? It's Doris who will be asking him," Christine taunted her, staring at her.

"She means—why should he not? This is happening in the kingdom he is going to be the king of, and it's his responsibility to take care of it and its people. The coronation is a mere celebration." Doris felt bad about the way Christine said this, even though she couldn't understand her reason. But she didn't want to bring it up there.

"Do anything to bring back my daughter," Martha said.

"Okay, let's go then," said Doris.

"All right, I will go with them. John, take care of Martha. I will be back soon," Adyren said to her son and left with Doris and Christine for the castle.

The castle glowed with lamps that could be seen from a distance, as such arrangements were done.

"I sense Cherry is here nearby," Adyren said, feeling alert.

"What?" Doris was surprised and found it crazy.

"Yes, she is in trouble too," Adyren said, worried.

"Weird," Doris murmured, and Christine heard her but didn't react or say anything in response.

As they arrived at the gate, they could see that it was crowded within.

"Hm, good evening, Mister. I am Doris Wilson. I want to see the king," Doris said to a guard at the door.

"Sorry, miss, but I am afraid that his Majesty Edward is too busy right now to see people such as yourself. Please come on the day of the coronation to see him," the guard replied.

"What? Who do you think we are? We have not come here to have a glance at him like other silly girls." Doris felt offended.

"You do not look like some princess either by your attire," the guard mocked.

"I blame Christine for that. But how dare you speak like that to me?" Doris was angry now.

"Hm, we are sorry on her behalf, but we really are in need of help. Her granddaughter has been missing the whole day. We would be grateful if you'd let us meet the king." Christine stopped Doris from speaking anymore and tried to speak out about their problem.

"I understand that, but I can't help you with this. I am quite busy handling the guests. Now, will you please excuse me?" the guard said, ignoring them and welcoming a chariot that had just arrived.

"I will get you fired if you do not listen to us," Doris shouted in front of the guests who alighted from the chariot.

The guard felt embarrassed and angry as well. He asked his fellow guards to throw them out from there. As they approached her, Doris saw the real Joseph inside.

"Edward!" she shouted, waving her hand.

Joseph saw her and immediately hid himself. When the guards turned, they couldn't see him, so they got angrier. The ladies were thrown out from there.

"Oh, you morons! Now, you will pay for this," Doris shouted as the guards left.

"Yeah, I am scared," one of the guards said while walking away.

"Great. Thanks to you, Doris, we're not going to get any help from them. Why would you want to cause any more troubles in our lives?" Christine said, frustrated.

"You blame me for this?" Doris asked.

As they started to argue again, Cherry's grandmother began chanting something.

Doris noticed her, but before she could say anything, she saw Lord Fitzgerald from a distance with a few men going toward a nearby isolated glass hall outside the castle.

"Lord Fitzgerald!" Doris shouted to him.

Adyren and Christine started to follow Doris, who followed Lord Fitzgerald since he didn't hear her.

"I want him dead tomorrow at any cost," Fitzgerald said to his men.

Doris felt alert and said nothing. She listened to what he was saying.

When Christine and Adyren reached her, she shushed them to prevent them from speaking and made them listen to him. So, they hid as well.

"But it is too crowded to kill the king," a man said.

All three of them felt astonished to hear this.

"I don't know anything. I have waited so long. I do not have any more patience. Regardless of how crowded it gets; we are to stick to our plans to kill him. I can't even stand seeing him wearing the crown. Just kill him when I indicate to you. It's going to be right here in this dining hall. All the guards in the hall area are on our side. He shouldn't get away from this," Fitzgerald said.

As they listened to Fitzgerald very carefully, someone caught them behind them, and they startled. He pushed them into the hall in front of Fitzgerald before they could make a run for it.

"I caught them listening to you hiding behind the door, my lord," the man said, standing behind them.

"Oh, look at that. We have company here. Oh, my dear Doris, how are you?" Lord Fitzgerald asked.

"Hey, Lord Fitzgerald, this man is lying. We didn't hear anything. We just followed you as the guards over there were not letting us in. But we didn't hear a word, really. Were you saying something?" Doris tried to behave as if she was unaware of what they were saying. Even though she knew it wouldn't help but it was worth a shot.

"Oh, is that so? We need to be careful when speaking about our plans now. I know you are very clever." Fitzgerald laughed and said. "Oh look, you sorted out your issues with Christine!" Fitzgerald continued, looking at Christine.

"What? How do you know we were fighting? Is it something you said?" Doris asked. "Is it because he said something to you, Christine? You just saw what a player he is! Did you not? How could you believe anything he says?" she asked, looking at Christine.

"So, you heard everything," Fitzgerald said. "Catch them all and throw them in the dungeon. They don't need to live anymore. I will take care of them after I am done with Edward," Fitzgerald commanded.

As the men came closer to catch them, Christine removed her gloves and said, "One more step, and I will turn you all into stone."

They ignored what she said, as they did not know what Christine could do. They walked closer, laughing, and the moment one man held Doris, Christine touched him, and he really turned into a statue.

Everyone felt shocked seeing that. Doris knew it but couldn't really believe her eyes, witnessing it in real.

"This cannot be possible. You cannot be alive!" Fitzgerald was astonished for some other reason.

Doris loosened her grip from the statue, and the rest tried to run.

"Catch them. I want them all at any cost," Fitzgerald commanded his men.

"She is a witch. We must kill her," they said.

Adyren was afraid to hear that. So many men tried to catch Christine, but she turned all of them into statues. Doris tried to fight as much as she could, drawing from her sword fighting lessons with Edward. One man approached her to cut Christine's hands off.

Doris and Adyren's hearts skipped a beat at the thought of losing Christine, but that man turned into a statue too. The men were frightened by her.

At last, somehow, one of them could catch her with a blanket and bind her.

Adyren chanted and got themselves unbound. It was this that shocked Christine and Doris along with the others.

"What the hell is happening here?" Doris exclaimed.

"Run, both of you!" Adyren shouted.

She cast a spell again and turned a man into a mouse. Before she could do any more harm, Fitzgerald hit her head hard from behind. She fell to the ground. The remaining men caught them again. They were afraid, imagining Doris could surprisingly do something too.

But somehow, they were all thrown into a dark dungeon.

"There is no way she was here all this while, right in front of my eyes, and I couldn't recognize her. How did I miss noticing?" Fitzgerald started murmuring loudly.

"Is anything bothering you, my lord?" a man asked. "They have been caught."

"Half of our men are statues now. Kill Edward tomorrow anyhow. I have more things to handle," Fitzgerald said concerned.

"What about these witches?" the man asked.

"You first concentrate on doing the job I asked you to," Fitzgerald said.

Chapter 19

The Dungeon

Joseph informed Edward that Doris was at the door looking for him, and he panicked. He also told him that she was with Christine, adding whatever she had said to him about Christine believing he was Edward and how Fitzgerald had told Christine everything. "I am sorry that I couldn't tell you about these things sooner. I've been too busy with this coronation thing going on lately," Joseph apologized.

"Oh my God! It's not your fault, Joseph. It's mine. I shouldn't have hidden this from her for so long. It was an unnecessary lie. I don't know why I did that. She must have heard about it and is definitely angry at me." Edward was worried.

"I think she doesn't know yet because she called me Edward. But it can be a problem if she hears about it now. Her friend is here too," Joseph said.

"Oh, seriously, what was going on in my mind that I lied to her about this? I must tell her now before I destroy everything at the

The Dungeon

coronation before introducing her to my mother. Where is she?" Edward asked him.

"She was at the gate," Joseph informed him and took Edward there.

"Where is she?" Joseph asked the guard.

"Good evening, Your majesty, my lord. Who in particular are you asking about?" the guard greeted and asked them.

"Doris. I mean there were two girls and an old lady here talking to you. She shouted 'Edward'," Joseph explained.

The guard took no time to remember her and was definitely scared recalling what he had done to them. "Yes, my lord. They just left. Who were they if I may ask?" the guard asked, hesitatingly.

"Oh, she is going to be your queen, if you must know," Edward replied with an anxious look.

"What?" The guard was more than scared now.

"Yes, and I want you to go and look for her. I need to talk to her," Edward commanded.

"Yes, sire, but guests are coming," the guard said, bowing.

"I will leave somebody else in charge of that. This is more important. She lives in a cottage in the middle of the forest, in case she has returned there. Bring her with all respect. Tell her that I apologize she had to return," Edward commanded.

This made the guard feel strange and afraid too. "Yes, Your Majesty", is all he said and went looking for her with his companions, hoping that she didn't go far.

Doris, Christine, and Adyren were thrown into different cells of a dark dungeon. Adyren was hit hard on her head and was still unconscious. Christine and Doris were afraid that she was no more.

"Aunt, wake up please!" Christine cried from the cell in the parallel front.

Doris shouted, hitting the door, "Let us go!"

"Christine is that you?" a voice reached her from the dark corner of the cell.

"Who is that? Cherry? Is that you?" Christine asked, recognizing her voice from the opposite cell. Doris turned to look and found Cherry in the same cell.

"Oh, thank God." Christine sighed and had a glimpse of Cherry from a distance in the dark.

"What happened to my grandmother?" Cherry cried, seeing her grandmother lying on the floor of the cell just next to theirs.

Doris went to the bars separating them, reached out, and tried to hold her head from between the bars, as it was bleeding. She dragged her closer and checked her pulse, which was still there. She tore a piece of cloth from her gown and tied her head where it was bleeding.

"Who did this? Why did they hit my grandmother?" Cherry cried again.

"Cherry, did you know that your grandmother could do magic?" Doris asked.

"Hm, who told you that?" Cherry was hesitant.

"That is why she was hit on her head. We saw it with our own eyes." Doris told her about what had happened.

"Yes, I saw her practicing once. She healed my pet bird when it was attacked by a cat, and I watched her. But she told me not to utter a word about it—otherwise, people would throw us all out of the kingdom and put us in a deep forest, like they did with Christine's mother. She said they would never let us return to town," Cherry told them.

"Oh, this little girl is a box of secrets!" Doris exclaimed. "You mean that she is a witch too?" Doris continued.

"Don't call her that. My grandmother never hurt anybody and has always helped people. She does not even practice it anymore. Just do something to bring back my grandma," Cherry cried.

"She will be all right. Don't worry, Cherry. Everything is going to be fine. She is alive." Doris was afraid too but tried to console Cherry. This was the first time Doris talked to Cherry in her politest way.

"She may feel better if we give her something to drink. Bring me some water. Would you?" Doris asked.

"Wait, are we going to get water at night?" Cherry asked.

"What do you mean?" Doris couldn't understand.

"They didn't give me water and said that I was going to die anyway," Cherry told her.

"You mean you have not even had water since you were put here?" Doris and Christine were surprised.

"Yes … and I am so thirsty now," Cherry complained. Doris noticed that her lips were pale and parched.

"And are they really going to kill you too?" Doris realized the gravity of what she had said.

"They said so," Cherry replied.

"He can't be so cruel. I never thought that he would be evil enough to kill a child! Everyone and everything were so sweet since I got here. It was like a town of sugar. How can it turn upside down over here so suddenly, and how can everything go so bitter?" Doris was worried.

"That is how people appear from the outside. You can never tell who is evil inside," Christine mused out loud.

Doris heard her. "Really? You want to start this now? What have I done to you that you won't stop taunting me today?"

"Please don't fight. I am already scared enough," Cherry interrupted them.

"Oh, Cherry, nothing is going to happen. We will get out of here," Christine said.

"I don't think that is possible. There is not even a single person to guard us, so we could trick them. We *are* going to die, Christine." Cherry knew the truth.

"How can you talk about death so easily? Do you even know what it means?" Doris asked.

"Grandma always said that when good people die, they go to heaven, which is a very good place. And if she ever died, I should not worry and only feel happy for her. I think I will go to the same place too if I die," Cherry said innocently.

Doris and Christine felt bad she was trapped with them. She was too little to die, in case they couldn't escape.

"This is the worst day of my entire existence!" Christine cried.

"God, why the hell are you all crying? Give it a break. Let me think of something!" Doris yelled.

"How will you help here?" Christine asked.

"Well, I don't know, but you are not helping in any way either!" Doris yelled again.

Cherry started to cry again. "Why are you fighting?"

Doris held Cherry close to comfort her, staring at Christine.

"Wait, but how did you end up here?" Doris asked Cherry.

"When I took you to king Edward—I mean Joseph. I started looking at the arrangements that were being made. It looked so beautiful, so I started wandering around. It was then that I heard lord Fitzgerald planning the murder of the king, and he saw me and threw me in here. I heard that he was the one who killed the king." Cherry told them everything that had happened.

"I can't believe that Joseph's father is behind this entire thing. I can't believe that I even talked to him and couldn't smell his evilness. I am worried about my Joseph," Doris said.

"Oh, stop it, Doris. The one you were with was not Joseph. It's king Edward who you love." Christine couldn't stand the confusion Doris had.

"Look, Christine, I don't want to start that. You need to—"

"You need to know people first. The one you love is Edward and not Joseph," Christine interrupted.

"Oh, is that so? Well, ask Cherry then. She is the one who takes me to him daily. Tell her, Cherry," Doris said to Cherry.

"Hm, Christine is right, Doris." Cherry's words shocked Doris.

"Look, Cherry, I know that you don't like me, but this is not the time to take revenge for all of it," Doris said.

"I am telling you the truth. It's king Edward you always meet. He just hid it from you because you spoke against the prince the first day right in front of him and you assumed he was not the prince, and I don't know why he continued going with this lie all this while, but the truth is that it is Edward you love," Cherry explained.

Doris was shocked to finally understand why Christine was mad at her and wondered what would happen now. Betraying her friend was not an option, but leaving Edward wasn't possible too. She realized the depth of the dilemma she was in and just sat quietly.

The guards sent by Edward, were tired of looking for Doris everywhere, returned to the king, and told him that things at the cottage were completely broken. Edward smelled some danger and immediately ran to look for her. When he saw that it was true, he was afraid and went to town to look for her. He sent his men to look for her in the forest at night too. The guards now regretted throwing them out and got themselves stuck in extra work. When he went into town, he found Cherry's parents on the way and learned that Doris along with Christine and Adyren had not returned after they had left to meet him.

"Oh, Doris, where might you be?" Edward started to worry about her, leaving all his work at the castle.

"Hm, sire, we apologize, but maybe she is still in the castle trying to look for you, and you are here. I think we must look there too," a guard suggested.

"I think you are right. She is Doris. When you didn't allow her in, she must have tried to get in somehow, evading your sight. She wouldn't leave without meeting me if she had made up her mind to meet me." Edward felt a little relieved and went back to his castle, hoping to find her there. But he could never imagine she would be in a cell. When he returned, he asked his men to look for her and unwillingly got busy with his guests.

In the dungeon, Doris felt like crying but held back her tears. She felt guilty and wondered how Christine would be feeling about her. They both did not say anything.

"I miss my mother and father. I want to see them before they kill us," Cherry said when the silence and dark started to scare her more.

"Oh, Cherry, don't talk like that. We are here for you. We surely will figure out something," Christine said, observing Doris lost in her thoughts.

Cherry's grandmother woke up. She saw Cherry and hugged her immediately through the sidebars separating their cells. She was furious that Fitzgerald had even taken her granddaughter but was too weak to speak about it. But at least that gave the others, a little hope of escaping with the help of her magic. She tried to open the door of the cell with her magic. But Fitzgerald was clever enough. He decided, since she was a witch, to trap her in a special cell so that she wouldn't escape with her magic if she returned to consciousness. The ground of that cell had strange engravements which somehow thwarted the use of magic. One of the walls of that cell had talismans stuck on it which Adyren was not able to touch without burning her skin. Fitzgerald had learnt a thing or two to capture a witch if he ever found one, for some reason which came handy that day to him. Adyren tried hard but was only disappointed.

They slept hungry, thirsty, and tired after the long day they had had. Cherry slept on Doris's lap, which she never even thought would happen.

Chapter 20

The Lost Princess

It was finally coronation day. After a long time, the queen mother was happy that day. Edward was excited too. Every expected guest had arrived even in such short notice, and the environment in the kingdom was lovely. People were happy, and it was like Christmas all around.

However, Lord Fitzgerald was hiding from one particular guest—someone from his past—meeting whom was probably inevitable at this event.

Doris, Christine, Cherry, and her grandmother woke up fearing for the life of the prince followed by theirs. It was just the day they needed to do something.

"Oh my God, I never thought I would be so worried on the day of Jo—I mean, Edward's coronation," said Doris.

"We must do something." Christine was panicking too.

"I am thirsty," said Cherry, with parched lips.

"Oh, my poor little girl, I wish I could do something. But I do not understand why my magic is not working in here. I am so sorry, my girl," Cherry's grandmother said helplessly.

"You don't need to be sorry, Grandma. It's not too bad," Cherry said, with a smile so that her grandmother wouldn't feel bad for her.

"How come you've been able to do magic all this while and kept that a secret from all?" asked Doris.

"We were three sisters. Me, Julie, who was Christine's foster mother, and Sophie—all of us could do magic," Adyren informed.

"You have one more sister? Mother never told me that," Christine said.

"We *had* one more sister," Adyren corrected.

"Oh, I am sorry, Aunt. But what happened to her? Why did you both never mention your sister to me?" Christine wanted to know about her other aunt.

"Sophie was the youngest and dearest sister to us. She fell in love with a prince during our journey and married him. She was so beautiful that the prince couldn't resist her beauty and married her. He loved her so much too, and we were heartily glad for her. We raised her as our own child, as she was far younger than we were. She, however, was always afraid that her husband would find out about her sorcery. And that's why she never revealed her real identity to her husband and swore never to practice magic.

"She told us that she tried indirectly asking her husband many times how he would react if she could do magic. But her husband never appreciated that and only showed hatred toward those who could do magic and called them witches. That made Sophie decide that she would never tell her husband about her being what he called a witch. I, however, had married here too, but my husband knew about it all, appreciated me, and loved this thing about me. Julie was the troublemaker for us all. She never wanted to quit it and wished that she could find a husband like mine. She loved being able to do magic. Well, who wouldn't? But she never found somebody who would love a witch. I was quite lucky in that case."

"Once she went to visit Sophie, and since she couldn't resist doing any magic, she got herself into trouble because of that. Sophie's brother-in-law was the king of that kingdom, and he had just had a baby girl. Fitzgerald was one of the brothers of the king too." Adyren told them the story.

"Hold on—Fitzgerald? This Fitzgerald? He was a prince?" Christine didn't know that.

"Yes, he was Sophie's brother-in-law. But I don't know why he ended up here. It was because of him that Julie's identity was exposed before the townspeople, and she was exiled. I volunteered to go with her, but she refused, as I had a perfect family over here and Fitzgerald never knew me. But I promised to always look after her and you from here," Adyren added.

"Woah! I have been here for so long but am learning of the interesting stuff now." Doris was curious.

"Yes, because we never got time to sit peacefully and talk about things. Also, we never spoke about Lord Fitzgerald, and his story did not come up," Adyren said.

"I have been living here my entire life, yet I was never told about this." Christine complained. Adyren couldn't say anything to Christine.

"Then, what happened, Grandma?" Cherry was curious to know about her grandmother and her sisters too.

"Oh yes, the king had a baby girl. Being the first child in the family, she was the apple of the entire family's eyes right after she was born. The prince, Sophie's husband, being her uncle, loved the child the too. One day, Sophie and Julie were alone in Sophie's room with the baby princess, or so they thought. Julie was cleaning the baby princess's mess with magic and wasn't letting Sophie clean it up with her hands. Sophie warned her that someone might see. And unfortunately, that day, Sophie's husband saw things flying around with his own eyes. He shouted immediately and gathered everyone at the castle at that moment and blocked their route to escape. Anyway, Julie was the one who could run away if she wanted to, but where could Sophie have gone? It was her home then. Julie asked her to escape with magic, but Sophie didn't agree as she loved her husband so much. And that persuaded Julie not to run from there, leaving her dear sister in trouble too.

"Sophie's husband asked who was doing magic, but before Julie could say something, Sophie said it was her, thinking that her husband would spare her, but not her sister. But she was wrong. The queen asked for her baby back without any harm. Sophie cried that she didn't mean any harm to her and that baby was like her own baby. But nobody believed her. Her husband tricked her, making her believe he would not cause any harm to her and Julie. He somehow went closer to her to take the baby princess, and our innocent Sophie believed that her husband couldn't do anything wrong with her. She allowed him to take the baby from her hands.

"Julie cautioned her not to let him go near her as he seemed angry, but Sophie said, 'No, Julie, he loves me. He doesn't mean any harm to me. He is just startled watching us do magic.' But the moment he took the baby, he stabbed Sophie to death. Sophie died, overcome with disbelief and broken faith right in front of Julie. Julie was so furious to watch her baby sister die that she snatched the baby princess from the prince's hands and shut everyone out of the room. They could see Julie and the princess, but they couldn't step inside the room because of the magic. She cried beside Sophie's body, told them that we loved our baby sister with all our hearts, and admonished them for killing her just because she could do magic.

"She never intended to cause any harm to anybody and even sacrificed her capabilities of doing magic for her love—only to be murdered by her husband. It was something that was unforgivable at that moment. She wanted to give them the pain she felt that moment, so she did something terrible out of pain. She cursed the princess, as she was the reason for Sophie's death. She cursed the princess that—" Adyren told them her own story and got emotional talking about her long-lost sister.

"What did Julie curse the princess with, Aunt?" Doris asked when she went silent for a while.

"Why are you silent, Aunt?" Christine asked too.

"She said they must realize how helpless we were for being able to do magic and that it wasn't up to us. She wanted them to realize how it felt when people hated and feared us and killed our sister because of something that wasn't even her fault. And that was only possible if someone closest to them all would similarly be feared and hated by all, without it being her fault, like in Sophie's case. So, she cursed the baby princess with the power to turn whoever she touched into a statue." Cherry's grandmother finally told them the truth, of which Christine had always been unaware.

Christine was too shocked to say anything when she realized that the woman she had always thought of as her mother was the one who cursed her with the hell of a life she had experienced.

"No way! You mean Christine is that baby princess? You mean Christine is a real princess!" Doris asked with wide eyes.

Adyren nodded in a guilty affirmation. Christine fell to the ground, overcome with disbelief. Cherry was surprised too.

"Oh my God. I am so sorry, Christine, for whatever is happening to you," Doris said, looking at Christine and realizing that moment was not the time to be joyous about Christine being a princess.

She didn't say anything.

"I wish I could do something. I wish I could hug you right now, Christine. I can literally feel you, and I am so sorry that this happened to you," Doris said, looking at Christine with wet eyes, as she could understand what she might be feeling.

"How did Christine end up here? What happened next? Did Julie kidnap her?" Doris had questions.

Adyren felt too sorry to say anything further.

"You must tell us! What happened next?" Doris insisted.

"After Julie cursed Christine, She dropped the spell, which allowed everyone to walk in. When Sophie's husband entered and held the baby, he turned into a statue right there. Everyone freaked out seeing what happened to the prince right in front of their eyes. But Julie never took Christine from there. She just took Sophie's corpse, flew from there, and swore never to return to that place ever again. After all, there was no reason to return. She came here and started to live with me. One day, when she was wandering in the forest to practice magic, as she used to, she heard the voice of a baby crying. When she followed the voice, she found the statue of a lady with a baby girl in her hands. Julie took no time to realize that the baby was the same she had cursed. She brought Christine back with care and thought of raising her as her own child. We thought that her family didn't accept her after the curse. Maybe they were afraid of her. So, we decided to keep her as our own child as we felt guilty and sorry for her too. Julie found a purpose in her life and fell in love with the baby herself," Adyren told them about what happened next.

"But she never fixed me? Even you didn't. You knew everything all along, but you still watched me suffer. What did I do to you both? I barely knew what was happening around. How could she curse me? She kept me all this while but never tried to fix me? She showed me that she loved me the most, but she let the curse stay in me and did not even try to fix me. And so did you. I can't hate you both more." Christine finally spoke in anger with tears in her eyes.

"She did, my child," Adyren said.

"Oh please …" Christine didn't want to listen to her anymore.

"How can she be fixed?" Doris asked.

"Julie put a curse on her that no witch can fix. Later, even though we tried to break the curse, we couldn't succeed. So, she cast the spell again but with a little modification: whoever truly loved her even after knowing about her curse and asked for her hand in marriage will be able to break the curse," Cherry's grandmother told them.

"And you claimed that she loved Christine? Why would she give such a complicated break for the curse when she could modify the spell in a simpler way?" Doris questioned her.

"There was a reason behind that. Julie didn't want her to end up with a person like Sophie's husband. She wanted her husband to be able to accept her even with her flaws—a person who would not just love her outer beauty but cherish her for her nature and respect her flaws too. And if who she met was not like that, he had better turn into a statue. That's what Julie wished for her, being a protective mother," Adyren explained.

"Protective mother?" Christine laughed, taunting.

"Still, this doesn't help me understand. You have created a huge mess out of her life. You are all not as sweet as you first appeared," Doris said.

"Well, they killed our baby sister, who we raised as our daughter. She was furious at that time. I might have done the same too if I were there. We tried to bend the curse, but it didn't bend in any other way but this." Adyren maintained her stance.

"Just tell me one thing, will you?" Christine asked Adyren.

"Yes, my girl, anything," Adyren said.

"You never told me about this. So, why now? Why did you tell me about this now and make me hate the only person I thought truly ever loved me?" Christine asked.

"She really loved you, Christine, and we all in here love you. Trust me," Adyren said.

"I am not sure who to trust anymore," Christine said with disappointment.

"I am telling you all this now, because in case we do not make it out of here, you deserve to hear the truth of your life," Adyren said.

"I deserve to hear the truth? Really! You think so? I have been here for seventeen years, unaware of my origin and knowing such few people growing up until she died. I had to earn money for myself when every other friend of mine was happily getting married. All this while, I have been afraid to fall in love with anybody. But I always thought that I was lucky to have a mother like her and I had you who always looked out for me even though I lived alone.

It's like everyone I ever trusted is a cheat! I don't even feel like living anymore." Christine was angry at everybody.

"Don't speak like that, Christine. I am really sorry. As for me, I never knew he was Edward. I swear to God. I don't even know why Edward did that, and if I knew, I swear I would never have gone so far with him. Please trust me," Doris said.

Christine didn't feel like talking to anyone.

The queen mother went to the hall to look at the arrangements and was mesmerized to see the decoration. "Oh my God, how did you make such beautiful arrangements in such a short time, lord Fitzgerald?"

"Why shouldn't I? It's going to be my coronation today," Fitzgerald murmured.

"I am sorry? I didn't quite catch you." The queen mother didn't hear what he said.

"I am sorry for not being audible, Your Majesty. I said, why shouldn't I? It's king Edward's coronation after all," Lord Fitzgerald said.

"Oh, we are so lucky to have you, lord Fitzgerald. It wouldn't have been so easy if you weren't here. Oh my, these statues look so real and amazing. It's like they could speak right now. Who made them? I would like to meet that artist." The queen mother was so amazed at seeing the statues of the people behind which Christine had a hand the night before.

"Uh, I am afraid that you cannot meet that person because we have had them imported from another kingdom," Fitzgerald said.

"Oh … but this is something nobody would have seen. I am sure he was paid well. I am so happy with your work, Fitzgerald. It must have been really hard on you. I suggest you take a long leave to rest after the coronation." The queen mother admired him.

"Sure, Your Majesty, I will relax after the coronation," Fitzgerald said.

The Celebration

*I*t was evening, and the celebration had started. People began to come.

But there was complete silence in the cell. Christine felt cheated by all, and Doris and Adyren were silent out of guilt. It was like they had all given up even trying to escape. Cherry was really thirsty and hungry, because she had been there longer. But she wasn't saying anything as she could see that the conversation had turned sour. But the poor girl couldn't hide it for long. She fainted because of thirst and hunger.

"Cherry!" Doris shouted, hearing a thump when she fell to the ground. Christine and Adyren also stood concerned, seeing Cherry from their respective cells.

"Cherry! What happened to my girl?" her grandmother shouted, crying upon seeing Cherry on the ground.

"Hello, is anybody there? You can't do this! There's a kid in here. Have some heart at least. Hello?" Doris shouted at the top of her voice, hitting the bars of the cell.

Cherry's grandmother was furious at Fitzgerald now because his capture of her granddaughter had led to her present condition. She tried her best to do some magic but only failed at it.

A guard at the main door of the jail could hear them screaming, and he was afraid of them so he had not gone to them so far. But at this moment, he couldn't stop himself from checking on them anymore.

"What is it? Why are you all shouting?" asked the guard of the jail.

"Are you really human? You have kept her here since yesterday and haven't even provided her with water to drink. She is so little and can't go through this. You don't seem like a person with a heart to me," Doris said angrily.

"You are all witches. If I provided you with water, you could use it against me with some trick." The guard replied.

"I am the only witch in here. Please give her some water at least. I beg you to show some mercy on her," Cherry's grandmother pleaded.

"Liar! I saw that one turning men into statues. You are all witches." The guard wanted to help them by giving water at least but feared them.

"That is me. Those two in there are normal. Just give them water if you fear us both. Please, I beg you," Christine beseeched.

"All right, but I don't want any cleverness in here with this. Otherwise, it wouldn't be good," the guard warned them.

"Yeah, we promise," said Christine.

The guard brought some water and gave it to all of them. Doris splashed some water on Cherry's face and fed her some while being unconscious. The guard also looked at Cherry.

The moment Cherry returned to a little consciousness, her fingers moved involuntarily while she still lay on Doris's lap, and water started to emerge from an unknown source within their particular cell. The entire floor soon turned wet while Cherry kept saying, "Water! Water!" Doris looked around to find water all around her. Christine and Cherry's grandmother were astonished too.

"Witch, she is a witch too!" The guard got frightened and moved back without thinking close to Christine's cell. Christine's sight fell on the keys in his pocket, and she tried to take it out from there while he looked at Cherry. But soon, he noticed a hand coming toward his pocket, so he turned and accidentally touched Christine's hands out of anger to try grabbing the keys. And account of the curse, he turned into a statue too.

Doris saw this and stood. "Oh, thank God. Search for a key, Christine. There must be something to get us out of here."

"There is no key in his pockets," said Christine.

"Oh, how do we get out now?" asked Doris.

"With the help of this," Christine said, showing them the keys in her hand.

"Oh, you …" said Doris with happiness.

The Celebration

They somehow escaped the cell and ran toward the castle.

At the gate, the same guard was standing who had not allowed them to go through. "Oh, there you are, Ms. Doris! We found you finally." The guard sighed with happiness, but they panicked, assuming he could be on Fitzgerald's side, and ran inside.

"But wait, I am really sorry. Please don't tell the prince—hm, the king," the guard shouted from behind them.

"King Edward has chosen her?" the other gaurd asked.

"Oh, don't say that out loud in case he hears us. We would both be out," the guard replied.

They had to avoid anyone in a uniform, as they might be on Fitzgerald's side, and they were not sure whom to trust anymore.

Fitzgerald had noticed that his brother and sister-in-law, who were also Christine's parents, were also there, and hence, he hid. And that made him more worried.

"My lord, they are not in the cell. I saw James's statue at the entrance of the dungeon when I was passing by and went inside to find Logan near the open cell, also turned into stone. They are all out," a man said to Fitzgerald.

"What? Oh no, no. This can't be happening. Her parents are here. I can't risk anything today. Everything is going wrong. I should have killed them all yesterday. Find them before they spoil everything, and kill them. They should not reach Edward at any cost. Be by his side all the time, so they don't get to him. Oh my God, this is a nightmare." Fitzgerald was angry as well as anxious now about his plans. He started to become more desperate.

In the meanwhile, Edward asked Joseph about Doris in his room. There were maids all around to get him ready.

"Oh God, I can't get out of this. Please bring Doris to me the moment you see her. I need to talk to her," Edward said to Joseph while stuck in there.

"I can't find her, Edward. I have asked our men to look for her. There is no sign of her." Joseph had already looked.

"I feel like seeing her and asking her how I look. I want her to be by my side. It is a very important day of my life, and I so want her to be with me right now." Edward missed Doris.

"Oh, my dear friend, she will be here soon," said Joseph.

"I hope so. I just hope she hasn't found out the truth from somewhere else. And I am afraid of this just because she wasn't home last night. I couldn't even meet her last night. What if she is mad at me and left?" Edward was afraid. He wasn't aware that Doris was missing. He just assumed that he couldn't meet her and that she would be home later.

"She cannot be that mad at you that she would leave you behind on this day that matters so much to you if she truly loves you. Don't think so much." Joseph calmed him down.

"Oh Joseph, it would be my honor then to have you as my best man," said Edward with a little sense of relief.

Fitzgerald tried to make a plan to avoid any problems later. He went to the queen mother somehow and told her that there were a few witches at the castle but hiding.

The Celebration

"What? What are you saying, lord Fitzgerald? Do witches really exist?" She couldn't believe this.

"How are you not aware that they exist, Your Majesty? My own brother was killed by one. I have seen a few with my own eyes. And I got news that a few witches escaped our captivity," Fitzgerald said.

"What? When did you capture one?" the queen mother asked.

"Last night, Your Majesty. I couldn't inform you, as you were really busy with guests. I saw them doing magic with my own eyes," Fitzgerald said.

"Oh my God! Why are they here? What do they want from us?" the queen mother asked, worried.

"I don't know, Your Majesty, but they were planning to kill Edward, and I heard them. They were the ones who killed the king! And one of them is Doris, the woman our naive Edward is so madly in love with," Fitzgerald said.

"This can't be true. No, no, no! I can't believe this." The queen mother was furious to hear about the killer of her husband and that her son's life was at stake.

"I must show you then when we catch them, but I just want you to be careful. Don't let them go near the king." Fitzgerald was cunning. He immediately planned to blame Doris, Christine, and Adyren for murdering Edward after killing them.

"I won't let anybody touch my son then. And if they really intend to harm my boy, they must go through me. Inform our staff to be aware of them. The guests must not be troubled, but get all our men to work. Provide extra security to Edward so that nobody reaches him. Get me that girl first if you find her. I need to have a word with her." The queen mother found it hard to believe Fitzgerald, but she couldn't risk the life of her son.

"Sure, Your Majesty." Fitzgerald was now happy to see the queen mother was getting all the staff, whom he couldn't buy, to his side.

One of the men who was asked to look for Doris by the king and Joseph saw Doris and called her from a distance again. But when Doris saw him, she ran away to hide with all. Basically, every man was looking for her, but some were on Edward's command and some on Fitzgerald's.

Doris, Christine, Cherry, and her grandmother hid inside the queen mother's room.

"Oh my God, look at that! It's so amazing," said Doris.

Christine and Cherry looked at the dresses and accessories belonging to the former queen.

"I feel ashamed to wear what I'm wearing to this party. No matter how much trouble we are in, we must dress nicely, so that even if we die, we won't die ugly. If I wear this gown for long at this amazing high-society party, I will die anyway. I don't even want to be seen by anybody in this tatty old dress I'm wearing. Even servants are wearing better," Doris complained, holding her gown.

They decided to do a makeover so they wouldn't be identified easily in their old dresses at the party.

The Celebration

"But we can't steal the queen's clothes." Christine felt afraid when her moral conscience began to demand better of them.

"Not if I produce one," said Adyren. She chanted and put both Christine and Doris in nice, beautiful ball gowns.

"Oh, this is so beautiful, Aunt. I feel so nice." Christine forgot about all her anger for a moment but then suddenly went silent when she recalled that she was mad at her.

"Oh, yeah. Now we're talking. What is magic for if you can't get yourself party-ready at the last moment? I want Ellis to see me now," said Doris and then realized that Christine was also there. She had one other thing to sort out as well, in addition to saving him and themselves.

"What about me, Grandma?" said Cherry, looking at them in wonder.

"Oh, how can I forget my own little princess?" Cherry's grandmother said and put Cherry in a cute little dress too.

Being girls, what else could they have wanted at such a bad time to lighten their moods?

In one of the castle corridors, all the men were told to keep looking for the four. The guests were enjoying their time, but the men were at work.

Joseph also looked for Doris as he was asked by Edward, and he saw his father up to something. He stopped a man and inquired what the rush was about.

"There are four witches in the premises willing to kill his majesty. We must protect him but not tell him," the man replied.

"What? Who?" Joseph asked.

"One of them is the girl the king met on a regular basis. I guess her name is Doh … Doris, yes, Doris. That's the name. There is a young girl, an old woman, and one more girl of her age with Doris. He said that they escaped jail," the man explained.

"What rubbish! Who told you this?" Joseph inquired.

"Lord Fitzgerald. And we were asked to provide extra security to his majesty, so she does not reach him. This is happening by the order of the queen mother," the man informed Joseph.

Joseph let him go and immediately went to his father. "What are you cooking up now, Father?" Joseph asked Fitzgerald all furious.

"Nothing, my son," Fitzgerald said with a smile.

"Then, why are you spreading this news that Doris is a witch? You know she is not," Joseph said.

"She is not indeed, but the women along with her—Christine and the old lady—are. I ask you not to worry yourself over these matters and enjoy the evening. Look, your fiancée Katherine is also here. And what kind of gentleman are you to leave your woman alone at a celebration like this? What must she be thinking?" Fitzgerald asked his son.

"Oh, don't bring Katherine into this, Father. I know you so very well. I have never said anything to you since you are my father, but Edward is going to be coronated today and is very happy. I do not want any kind of trouble today. And you had her captured in the dungeon last night? If Edward finds out about this, you will see the worst of him." Joseph knew that his father's intentions were never good yet he tried to warn him.

"I know what I am doing, Joseph, and you better leave me to my work. Otherwise, I will have to forget that you are my son," Fitzgerald said in a grim tone of voice and left.

Joseph didn't waste any time, ran to Edward, and told him everything, omitting the fact that his father held her in the dungeon. But Edward understood that this had something to do with Doris having gone missing the previous night. He rushed to his mother to talk about this. When he came out, people started to hail him. Doris, Christine, Cherry, and her grandmother heard them from the room they were hiding in and got to know that Edward was out. They could trust nobody but him, so they had to reach him somehow.

Edward went to his mother through the crowd and asked her what was happening.

"Edward, you must be careful. Don't even stand without guards around you. There are witches who killed your father and intend to kill you. Lord Fitzgerald told me that Doris is one of them, and he saw her with his own eyes and had her captured in the dungeon, and she escaped that too," his mother told him.

"What? Doris was in the dungeons last night? How dare he? I am not going to spare him. I asked him to stay away from me and Doris. Where is he?" Edward was furious.

"Edward, son, it's your coronation today. You must not think of anything else. And see, everyone is looking," the queen mother said, looking around at the people watching them.

"No, Mother. I know it's my coronation, and I was so excited too because I am going to have a huge responsibility on me. But that doesn't mean that I will bear seeing Doris being tortured for no reason. And she is no witch. I have known her the most. Lord Fitzgerald knows nothing."

"Okay, let's go to your room and talk about this. What will people say? They must not hear that there are witches," his mother tried to calm him down.

"Why don't you understand, Mother? She is not a witch!" Edward raised his voice, and the people around them looked at them. The queen mother held his hand and took him to his room like a kid. Edward thought that she was going to talk, but the moment he entered, his mother locked the door and asked the guards outside to let him out only when it was time. She then asked the others to look in every room and find them as soon as possible.

Edward was nothing but angry at both his mother and Fitzgerald.

The Curse

Doris and Christine peeked out for a chance to run to Edward. They saw that his mother took him and closed him in a room, with two guards at the door. It was crowded and not easy to reach the room, as it was across the hall on the upper floor.

"You can't do this to me, Mother," Edward shouted, banging the door from inside.

"I am so sorry, Edward, but your life is at stake. Please do understand and forgive me for this," the queen mother said from the other side of the door.

"It's not Doris even if there is someone out there to kill me. It can't be her, Mother. Don't hurt her," Edward said.

"I am sorry, Son. I lost your father. I can't risk losing you too," she said and left from there.

People started to watch what was happening.

"It is nothing. He is just panicking. Please enjoy the evening. Sorry about the trouble," the queen mother said, facing her guests coming down from the stairs.

She ordered her staff to look everywhere and find them as soon as possible, as they couldn't have gone outside.

A few went to the former queen's room to check too. When Christine heard people coming toward them along with Fitzgerald, she started to panic.

"Oh, don't be afraid since there is a witch with you." Adyren chanted and made them vanish for a moment when the men came to check the very room, they were in.

"Bloody hell! Why did you not do this before?" Doris asked.

"Well, I am used to not doing magic. So, I had forgotten that I could do this," Adyren replied.

"You must be kidding me. If you can do magic, well, this is the time to use all of it—" Doris said.

"This is the right time. Edward is locked behind that door. It is the time for me to go and kill him and tell the queen that it was those witches who did it. Just cover me, so nobody sees that I am going in there." It was Fitzgerald talking outside.

"Hush!" Doris shushed everyone to listen.

"We need to do something. He is going to his room. I never knew he was so cunning," Christine whispered.

"Do something, Grandma. He is going to kill the king," said Cherry.

"Ellis... I mean Edward doesn't know that Fitzgerald is going to kill him. Somebody needs to go to him," Doris panicked.

"I will lock the door so it doesn't open," Cherry's grandmother said and locked Edward's door with a spell. "Well, he will be busy for some time now," she said again.

"I just wish I could go in there and talk to him," Doris said, sitting on the bed.

"Wish granted," Adyren said.

"Really?" Doris was excited.

"Yes. But you can't go past that door in this human form of yours. What creature do you wish to become?" Adyren asked.

Doris could see that Christine was feeling a bit low when that topic came up. So, she thought of sending her to Edward instead.

"Another creature? Do you really think I would become a rat or something to go there? No way," Doris said in an arrogant manner even though she could have done it.

"But sending you like this would be a little difficult and riskier," Adyren said.

"Well, I am not going then. Christine might," Doris said.

"What?" Christine asked.

"Come on, can you not do just this for your prince charming? You claimed to have loved him so much," Doris taunted her.

"Well, it's not about proving my love but about saving a life, and it surprises me that you cannot even do that for him." Christine felt very strange that Doris was being so picky at that moment.

"Well, then, why don't you become a mouse?" asked Doris.

"Oh, I will. Turn me, Aunt. I will go," Christine said to Adyren on being provoked on purpose by Doris.

"All right, I am going to turn you into a mouse so you can go there easily and quickly. The moment you get in there, I will turn you into your original self. You need to tell him about Fitzgerald as soon as possible, and within a moment, I will turn you both again into a mouse, so you can bring him along here too," Adyren instructed. "Are you ready?"

"Yes, Aunty," Christine said taking a deep breath.

She then turned Christine into a mouse.

"Oh my God! It really happened. You look so cute this way." Doris laughed at Christine.

Christine stared at her in her mouse form.

"Okay, I will not say anything. Go now, and save your love," Doris said.

When Fitzgerald reached Edward's room's door, he was unable to open it. The men also tried hard while avoiding people's gazes at the same time.

"My king, have you locked the door from inside? I am here to help you get out of here. Let me in," Fitzgerald said from outside.

The Curse

"It's better if you do not come before me, lord Fitzgerald. I happen to respect you, but I am really very angry at you right now," Edward replied from within.

"Oh, I am so sorry, your majesty. We just have a little misunderstanding. Let me help you come out. I beg your forgiveness." Fitzgerald was desperate to get in.

"I haven't closed it from inside," Edward replied arrogantly.

"You haven't?" Fitzgerald couldn't understand.

As a mouse, Christine then somehow managed to get in through the pipes from outside the castle walls and entered the room from a window. She saw Edward, went closer to him, and watched him being worried, which made her wish he could be hers. But she knew that he belonged to Doris now and thinking about him with that knowledge was not right. So, without wasting any more time, she bit him on his leg so he would notice. When Edward saw her, he shouted, "A mouse!"

Hearing that, Adyren turned Christine into her original form.

"Mouse? Why is this door not opening?" Fitzgerald was frustrated outside, trying to open it under pressure.

"What on earth!" Edward said with disbelief, looking at the mouse turning into a fine woman, whom he recognized.

"You ... I know you. You are Christine about whom Doris always talks. My mother was right! You are a witch. Where is Doris? What did you do to her?" Edward asked in fear.

"Who are you talking to, my king? Is someone in there?" Fitzgerald heard Edward talking.

"I am not a witch, your Majesty, and I need you to listen to me very carefully without wasting anytime. Lord Fitzgerald is going to kill you today and put the blame on us for it. He is the one who had killed your father too, and when we found out, he put us all in the dungeon. You need to trust me right now even though it looks like the other way to you at this moment. Doris is waiting too. Any moment now, we will both turn into mice, and you need to run with me. And remember not to touch my hands at any cost," Christine explained to Edward, whispering.

"What?" It was too much for Edward to digest at that moment. But the moment he said it, the door was being banged at to be broken. When Doris and Cherry's grandmother saw that from the room where they were hiding, she turned them both into mice. When the door opened, both Edward and Christine ran out the door. Fitzgerald looked inside the room from there and understood that the witches had a hand in this, and he commanded his men to catch the mice, judging that one of them was Edward.

The staff started to run to catch them. One of them approached the mice from the front and made them jump into the crowd. The guests started to panic seeing two mice in there. The queen mother was worried about the party and their reputation being spoiled.

"Oh, no. What do we do now?" said Doris, looking at the mess.

"Stay here," Adyren said and came out of the room to distract everyone.

When Fitzgerald noticed the old lady, he could not help but yell, "That's the witch! Kill her!" All the guests witnessed what was happening.

"Fitzgerald!" said a guest from whom he was hiding. But his word was inaudible to everybody because people were shouting and jumping to avoid being touched by the mice.

When some men tried to run toward Adyren, she extended her hand and gestured, resulting in them floating in the air.

People were astonished to see that, and it distracted them from the mice.

Adyren threw them in the air and did the same to whoever approached her.

"Lord Fitzgerald was right. They are really witches. Where is my son?" The queen mother had now seen evidence of Fitzgerald's claims and felt worried, noticing Edward's room's door open from down.

"You cannot catch me now, Fitzgerald. You have been so evil and rude to us lately," she said to Fitzgerald, holding a few men in the air and then throwing them too. Eventually, there were too many for her to handle.

Joseph did not know whom to trust now. He knew that his father was no good, but he saw a witch attacking his people, and that made her an enemy to be attacked.

Doris watched all of this and perceived that Adyren could be hurt now because there were so many trying to catch her.

"Look, Cherry. I need you to listen to me very carefully. I have been a really bad person to you, and there is no way possible that you will ever obey me. I completely understand that. But I need to go save your granny and Christine and Edward. And I really

really want you to remain inside, no matter what happens. Will you please do me this huge favor one last time?" Doris tried to make Cherry understand and stay inside.

"Yes, I will. Go save them," Cherry agreed.

"Well, that was easy," Doris said. She saw a sword on the wall of the room, took it, and came out.

Edward and Christine wanted to help but were stuck being mice, and Adyren was too busy to turn them back into humans.

Doris also came out and started to fight. The guests only watched from the edge of the hall.

"Turn them back, Aunt. Only Edward can help us out of here. I have your back. Turn them back," Doris said to Adyren with a raised voice.

The mice came running to them, and noticing them, Fitzgerald ran toward them to kill them before the people learned one of them was the king. But he was too late. Adyren turned them back into their original forms. The people could not have been more astonished.

"Edward," the queen mother said, gasping.

"I need all of you to stop!" Edward shouted.

Everybody stopped to listen to him.

"Man, I was so excited about this day, and it is completely ruined," Edward said in the way Doris used to speak, looking at her.

"I need an explanation for whatever is going on in here," Edward asked, looking at Doris and Christine.

"Ellis... I mean your majesty; Fitzgerald killed the king and is going to kill you too. When we found this out, he threw us in that dark dungeon and was going to kill us after he killed you," Doris said.

"They are lying. Can you not see that they are witches? What other proof do you need that they are the ones who are going to kill you?" Fitzgerald maintained his stance.

"Yes, I can do magic, but that does not prove that I mean you harm of any kind. You kidnapped my Cherry for which we had come here to complain, but we found out about your evil plans," Cherry's grandmother explained.

"Who do you think would trust you?" Fitzgerald asked.

"I would," said a voice from the crowd watching it all happen.

"Brother." Fitzgerald could not stop himself from uttering this word, seeing his brother along with his wife.

"Yes. Edward, he *used* to be my brother and tried to kill me and my little daughter for the throne, and this made me exile him from my kingdom. But while going, he took my daughter with him. And I do not have any doubt he must have killed your father and now is making an attempt on your life. Where is my ..." Fitzgerald's brother said. But before he could ask where his daughter was, Fitzgerald tried to attack him with his sword.

Edward stepped in between them with a sword to save him. That made the fight start again.

Fitzgerald's men started to run to catch Edward, but they had to fight Doris, Christine, and Adyren first.

They were fighting in their own way. Adyren was handling them all with magic. Doris was fighting with a sword the way Edward had taught her. Christine was turning her enemies into statues.

"Christine?" Her real mother took no time to recognize that it was her daughter.

Christine heard her too but didn't respond and kept fighting.

Half of the men who were not on Fitzgerald's side couldn't decide whom to fight, but they tried to protect their king.

The queen mother was broken and could not believe that it could be Fitzgerald.

Doris fought at Edward's side, and Edward felt good watching her fight so well. "I must say that I have taught you so well," Edward said while fighting.

"Oh, yeah? Well, I have my own talents too," Doris said, saving him from a person who was attacking him from the back.

"Oh, I love you and can't wait to marry you," Edward said, taking a break and holding her waist in the middle of the fight—but not for long, as there were so many intending to kill him. Doris said nothing and got busy.

Fitzgerald was so mad seeing his plan ruined by those women. He somehow managed to go near Christine, threw a blanket on her hands, and tied her.

"Enough with this madness, or I will kill this girl," Fitzgerald shouted, taking Christine hostage.

"Christine!" Doris exclaimed.

All the men on Fitzgerald's side held the people who fought against him.

"You would not. She is your own niece, Fitzgerald. You would not," Christine's father said.

"Oh, try me. You are my own brother, and I was going to kill you. Do you still think that I will spare this one? And why should I? She has always been the one to spoil my plans at the very last moment of becoming a king. I was going to kill her, but my wife was an emotional fool who stopped me, as we had Joseph who was just like her. And it was just because of Joseph that I wanted her to die. But when my wife got to know I was still going to kill her despite her asking me not to, she stole her and ran away to save her. And she was punished for what she did and for not listening to her husband. This girl turned her into a statue. I searched for her so much, but when I found her, she was just a mere piece of rock, and the child wasn't there. I thought some animal would have killed her and would have done my bidding. You exiled me. I was going to kill her then, so why not now?" Fitzgerald said, holding his sword against her neck.

"You cannot be my father. I cannot believe you are this way. You always said that you loved my mother so much!" Joseph cried listening about her mother.

"Joseph, not right now. Spare me your drama. I am only doing this for you," said Fitzgerald.

"Don't you dare say you are doing this for me. I don't need this. I was always happy with the friend I had and with the queen who loved me like her own son. This is what is important to me. Look at yourself. You had such a great family, and you betrayed them and lost everything. Forget about people loving you. I pity you for you are incapable of loving anybody," Joseph said to his father.

"I loved her. Even though I didn't listen to her and she didn't listen to me, I loved her. It broke my heart when I found she had turned to stone. It was only me who visited her statue on a regular basis and nobody else. I had that place covered with pillars so no animal would disturb her. And that made me promise to find Christine and kill her to avenge her death," Fitzgerald said to his son.

This reminded Doris of the place where she had fallen while entering this world. But she could not understand the logic behind it.

"I cannot believe you, Fitzgerald. My husband sheltered you and treated you so well. What must he have felt when you killed him? What kind of monster are you?" the queen mother said with a broken voice.

"Spare me your emotional lecture please. I happen to be a prince, and I wished to be known for generations as a king. I desire to be mentioned in the books. But here I am, serving you, fulfilling your demands, and wasting my life. I am so tired of you," Fitzgerald said.

"Please, Fitzgerald, spare our daughter. You need the throne and the crown, right? We surrender our crown to you and give you our kingdom. Just please don't hurt her," Christine's mother said.

"I am not some beggar to get a kingdom out of pity. What would people say about me then? How would they mention me in the books passing through generations? And oh, about your kingdom, I will take that too after I take over this place with my own power," Fitzgerald said to his sister-in-law. He was then about to slit Christine's throat, but just at the right moment, Doris stomped on the feet of the guard holding her and escaped his grasp. She hit Fitzgerald hard on his arm and released Christine from his grip. Fitzgerald shouted in pain, and Doris went to help Christine up after she fell, escaping his grip.

Fitzgerald could not be angrier at that moment, so he ran toward Doris to kill her.

"Doris!" Edward shouted from a distance, still being held by a guard.

When Doris turned, she saw Cherry standing in front of her.

"What are you doing down here? I asked you to stay hidden until I asked you to come out. Why don't you ever listen to me? And you wonder why I hate you!" Doris shouted at Cherry.

But Cherry fell to the ground. There was a sword in her back, and blood ran all around. Doris saw that Cherry had saved her from Fitzgerald's stabbing.

"Cherry!" her grandmother cried at the top of her voice.

Christine cried, taking her name too.

Doris didn't say anything but fell to the ground in disbelief. She couldn't believe that Cherry was dead. Everyone could feel the pain of a little girl being killed.

Cherry's grandmother was so furious that everything in the hall started to shake. The doors opened on their own, and it turned dark all around. Dried leaves started to creepily flow in.

Fitzgerald was now afraid and understood that the woman was angry. He stepped back, looking at what was going on around him.

"You have exceeded the quota of sins you can commit. You are nothing but an object with no heart who wants to be in the books lasting generations. Then, let me help you become the one thing you desire the most.

"May you turn into a book that nobody would ever want to look at.

"May you be passed through generations as you desire, and may nothing release you to your true form, be it wind, sea, or fire.

"Your soul shall be trapped in this book forever. The one who thinks you can be spared after listening to all the sins you have committed will be the only one capable of releasing you if it happens ever." Cherry's grandmother cast the spell that turned Fitzgerald into a book, which Doris could immediately recognize. It was the same one into which she had entered. It took her no time to understand that she had been inside the same book the whole time for the purpose of learning about his sins.

Everybody could only watch all of this happening, and there was nobody to even plead for forgiveness on Fitzgerald's behalf—not even Joseph.

Back to Reality

Even the people who did not know Cherry felt remorseful about her death. Christine, Adyren, and the townspeople who knew Cherry cried there. Edward knew her, so he felt shocked too. Doris just sat at her place, as everything that had happened to her started to make sense all at once, and she realized that the reason for her being there was finally over and she would be thrown out any moment now just like she was thrown into the book.

Suddenly, Adyren, unable to stand, fell and started shivering.

"Mother." Her son saw her and came toward her.

"What is happening? Are you all right?" Christine came to see her too.

"I am sorry, Christine, on behalf of Julie too. We indeed made your life very lonely and miserable," Adyren apologized.

"Don't say that. I am sorry for not understanding your part and your loss. People feared you all and killed your loving sister because they were just afraid of you, even when you meant them no harm. But what is happening?" Christine was worried.

"I think I am being punished for using my magic to curse somebody. We are not dark witches, so we have to pay a price for cursing someone if it affects an innocent's life," Cherry's grandmother explained.

"What! This cannot be true. Julie also cursed me, but she never paid for it. Did she?" Christine couldn't understand.

"Oh, darling, you don't know. Since you were cursed to make people afraid of you, she paid the price herself by experiencing the same thing. She never found any love in her life too. It was not her choice to stay away from other people. She was partially cursed with the consequences of what she cursed you with," Cherry's grandmother said, shivering.

Doris was nearby and heard all of this but did not know what to do or say at that moment.

"So, you mean turning Fitzgerald into a book will have you face some of its consequences too? Nevertheless, he was not an innocent man. He clearly killed your granddaughter and is guilty of the assassination of the king and many such sins. Why do you have to pay a price for cursing him? This isn't fair." Christine was surprised.

"I don't understand this much myself. I might have to protect the curse. I need to check whether he will exploit the powers he has attained through the curse," Adyren added still shivering in pain.

"What does that mean?" Cherry's father asked.

"It means, my son, that you must take care of yourself and Martha. I know nothing can fill the void left by Cherry, but I pray that you are both blessed with lots of kids and happiness in your lives. I may not be around anymore. Fitzgerald can escape this curse by manipulating the story, and he can use his powers in a bad way, by playing with people's minds. I need to keep an eye on him so he doesn't cheat by putting in it a wrong description of himself and break the curse. He does not deserve to escape this so soon." Cherry's grandmother felt so much anger that she didn't have any mercy to forgive him soon.

"This is madness. You don't have to do this. Cherry is gone, and nothing can bring her back. How does this even make anything better at this cost?" Christine didn't feel that it was right.

"I have lived long enough, Christine. It is not a choice anyway. Take care, Princess Christine. I pray that you are rid of this curse as soon as possible," Cherry's grandmother said.

Christine and Adyren's son started to weep at her side.

Slowly, Cherry's grandmother started to fade away into thin air, and there was nothing left. Nobody knew where she vanished. Everyone was astonished by this.

Doris was not sure what to feel or do. She knew that she couldn't be there anymore and would have to part from Edward. The way Cherry died for her right in front of her eyes also disturbed her. She worried about Christine at the same time, wondering what would happen if she were gone. Her thoughts were imploding her brain. All her new hopes and dreams had ended, and it was like she had returned to reality. For a while, she had accepted her life there, wishing for her to be trapped there forever. Sometimes, she asked herself what would happen if she had to return, but it did not look possible. Nevertheless, now that it was clear that it was not some place she got lost in, she realized that all that happened to her was a mere illusion or some mind game—not real in the least. But how could she think the same about her love for Edward, her friendship with Christine? Whatever the case was, she didn't want to be separated from Edward. For a while, she dreamed of being married to him and planning a future with him, forgetting where she had come from. And finally, when she was the happiest there, it all turned upside down. She couldn't move.

Edward somehow knew she was traumatized and tried to go to her and comfort her. But Doris just ran away with the book. Edward tried to follow her till the gate but then thought of giving her some time. Also, he had to manage everything that went wrong along with taking care of Cherry's demise. He had to make decisions about the people who had been involved in the killing of the king. The coronation was clearly called off for the day.

Christine sat beside Cherry's family and tried to hold them up but also watched all that was happening around her. She could understand how everything had turned so wrong. Christine's parents approached her and asked her to go with them after apologizing. But she asked them to allow her to be with Doris and Cherry's family for a few days.

Christine felt bad about her behavior and knew that Cherry's family needed her at that time. But she could sense that her friend was not fine either, so she approached Edward.

Back to Reality

She bowed to him and said, "Your majesty, I apologize for disturbing you in the middle of your work right now, but may I talk to you for a minute? You might not know me. I am Doris's friend."

"Of course, I know you, Christine. Doris talks about you all the time." Edward turned to face Christine, leaving the group of people he was surrounded by.

"Oh, that is my honor. I am really sorry for what happened here because of us, really," Christine said.

"I don't know what to say. I mean, forget about this. I should be sorry for Cherry. She just gave her life to save Doris, and her grandmother—she just vanished!" Edward replied.

"Yes. I can hardly hold myself for what all happened, but so can Doris. Shouldn't you be going to her? She needs you the most right now." Christine wanted him to talk to Doris.

"I want to. But there are so many things here that require my presence. I can't even imagine if it were Doris. Nevertheless, I cannot even accept that Cherry is dead. I don't know what just happened here. I can never be a good king. I don't know why I am saying this in front of you, but she was just a child and I couldn't even—" Edward's voice cracked while speaking.

"Oh, sire, please don't think that way. It was something that nobody could stop." Christine tried to console him.

"No, I could. It should have been me in her place. I failed to save both of them. I should have saved Doris. I was going to marry her. I could have saved Cherry if I were there." Edward felt guilty as he thought he could do something.

"I think you both need each other. I will speak to the queen mother myself that you need some time alone, but just go to her. Please." Christine wanted to hug him, as she couldn't see him cry but knew that she was not the one who should comfort him.

"I can't." Edward knew that people were looking for him.

"I know you will make a very good king, sire. You put your people above all, but something tells me that if you do not go after her, you may never see her again." Christine knew about the book and could understand everything in pieces.

"Why do you think that?" Edward asked in surprise.

"I am sorry, but I can't tell you that. So, I insist you go to her," Christine said and left to see Cherry's parents, who were leaving with the corpse.

Edward went to Joseph and asked him to take care of everything while he was gone for a short time. He asked him to go with a bunch of people to Cherry's place and help them with everything they needed. He said he would meet him there afterwards.

Chapter 24

The Goodbye

Doris went to the same place where she had arrived there the first time. The broken statue of the woman in the middle of the jungle, whom she knew now was Fitzgerald's wife.

"All right, Fitzgerald. Come out. Just come out, you rat!" Doris shouted at the top of her voice in the middle of the forest, but there was no one.

"I know it is you. You are the diary. So, stop hiding now. You are an animal! How could you do this to me? How can you just play with my entire life and expect me to release you from this curse? You deserved it, but I do not. Come out!" Doris was mad at him for obvious reasons. She was in a rage for what she was going to lose. "You don't deserve to be released from this curse."

"Doris!" Doris heard a voice from behind her and turned.

It was Edward. "Who are you talking to? And what are you doing here?" Edward asked her.

"You … you are not real. What are you?" Doris said, crying.

"What are you saying, Doris? It is *me—your* Ellis," Edward said, going closer to her.

"No, don't come any closer. This is a lie. This whole thing is a lie. Nothing is true here. Nothing has been this whole time. Oh, I will go crazy," Doris said, holding her head with both of her hands.

"Do not talk like that. I love you," Edward said approaching her and holding her shoulder.

"No. Do not say that. Everything has been an illusion. Tell me who you are. Fitzgerald? Don't tell me this has been you." Doris knew that he was not real.

"Why are you talking like that? I really love you. Look into my eyes and tell me this love does not feel real to you," Edward said, holding her hand.

"Oh, my sweet love, I wish you were real. However, you are not. Also, I do not belong to this place. Even if I did, Christine loves you more and is meant for you here." Doris could feel everything for real but did not know what to say.

"It is not my Edward, Doris." Christine arrived at that place too.

"What do you mean?" Doris was more confused now.

"He is not Christine's Edward." Christine turned into Adyren.

"What the hell is going on here?" Doris was afraid now.

"I am sorry, my child, that because of my curse, you are going through so much," Adyren said, coming toward her.

"Don't come any closer. Stop right there. Is this a joke to you? I do not want to stay here at all. Send me where I belong this very instant!" Doris was furious.

"That is not up to me, sweetheart. It is Fitzgerald who gets to decide. I just have the power to fix the story if he tries to manipulate it. I am not alive anymore to do any magic," Adyren explained.

"This can't be happening. What the hell is wrong with you both? He was evil, but you are not innocent yourself. Look at you! You did not just curse him. You cursed me along with him, for no fault of mine. What were you thinking?" Doris yelled at her.

"I was not thinking. I was simply furious at the loss of my little granddaughter. I do not expect you to understand it, because I know it is my fault. But I felt like destroying the whole world back then and nothing less. He killed my little girl right in front of me, and I could not do anything. I agree that my mere curse has affected many lives. And this is why I am suffering the effects of this curse too. We witches are not allowed to harm innocents, and if we do, we will be cursed too. All the witches pay a price for what they ask. While cursing Fitzgerald, I thought he was evil and deserved it. I was confused about why I was cursed too when he was not innocent. But later, I realized when he started picking people to free himself. My curse indirectly included many innocents. My mistake affected your life too, and I could not be sorrier about it." Adyren felt bad.

"I don't know what to do with this. I don't know whether you realize how much this will impact me. You took away a really important time in my life. My school is impacted. My career ahead will be impacted. I know I enjoyed my time and was not punctual at school, but this long gap! Even though I played it cool, I was serious about my life. And not just that—I started to love someone here who does not even exist in reality. You say Fitzgerald was heartless. What do you think about yourself? Do you have any idea how much I love him? I do not even have his picture with me. I love a man who lives way back in the past," Doris complained.

"Oh, Doris, I am truly sorry for what you are going through. I cannot imagine your heartbreak. I do not know what to say. We did not think that it would affect you this much. You seemed like a free spirit. We did not imagine that you would get so attached here," Adyren explained.

"Oh, wow. So, you picked me because I seemed heartless?" Doris's voice broke while she said this.

"No, Doris." Adyren tried to console her.

"No, you are right. That was such a great help. It clearly does not affect me at all." Doris could hardly stand on her feet. She reflected on how heartless she appeared to people. This truly broke her.

"Do not cry, my love." Edward's hand was on Doris's shoulder.

"Why are you not stopping him from showing love to me now? This is cruel. Is it not over yet?" Doris did not see the point of the puppet show that they were still running.

Adyren did not say anything.

The Goodbye

"Seriously, tell me one thing. Who is he really? Is he your puppet following your instructions to keep me trapped here? Was all the love and emotions he showed me from a script written by you both? Or is all of this just going on in my head?" Doris genuinely wanted to know.

"He is part of the illusion, Doris. Part of him is Edward indeed as he had to stick as close as possible to Edward's true role in the story. However, the feelings that you think he has for you are what you always dreamed of or wished for. He had all the emotions or reactions that you always wanted the person you love the most to have. This is why he understands you the most, and this is why he kept you bound here until the end. We thought this was the only way to keep you within the story without having you trying to escape all the time," Adyren said softly, as she knew what she had done was not right.

"I can't believe you two. You are both so messed up, and you put me in this hell. What do I do now with the knowledge that the man I love is a robot controlled by what I wanted him to do or feel?" Doris got on her knees and cried.

"Oh, Doris," Edward spoke again, seeing Doris cry and hugged her back, on his knees too.

"I want to go home. Please," Doris, closing her eyes, said to Adyren without looking at Edward.

"I deserve this hatred from you, Doris. I am sorry that because of me, you had to go through all of this. But I promise you that you are going to find true love in your real life. Whatever seed of love you have sowed over here shall arrive as the sweetest fruit in your real life. You will receive far more love there in reality than you have had here. This is a witch's blessing. May you get all the love that you wish for in real life, my child." Adyren blessed her with a long face, thinking of the damage that they had done to her.

Doris stood and said in anger, "I do not want your pity, and I do not want your magic spells doing anything for me out of here at all."

"This was no magic, my dear. This is my blessing. I know everything is going to be good from now on in your life," Adyren replied kindly.

"Very well. Now, how many times do I have to request you to get me out of here?" Doris asked, wiping her tears and showing her bold self.

"All right, Doris Wilsone. Goodbye. It has been really nice knowing you and spending so much time with you. However, I am very sorry for everything. We did not intend to hurt you for sure. There is one request though. I know that what we did to you is unforgivable but do try to put yourself in our shoes and try to understand the circumstances that made us do this," Adyren said her final words to her.

Doris did not respond.

"All right, Fitzgerald. Let her go," Adyren continued, speaking loudly at the air to Fitzgerald.

Doris could feel the wind starting to blow, and when she was ready to finally leave, she felt Edward's hands holding one of her hands. She probably wanted him to stop her from leaving. "Goodbye, Doris. I really loved you."

"Oh, my sweet love, I love you so much too. I wish you could be with me forever and you loved me the way I really wished you to. What would I do without you, honey?" Doris said with tears in her eyes and leaned closer to him to kiss him goodbye for the last time. The wind blew faster, as she in fact really kissed him for the last time.

Chapter 25

Back Home

Doris opened her eyes when she could no longer feel Edward and the wind. She found herself in Kate's room.

"I can't believe this! Doris, you are really back," Kate said, with tears in her eyes and a smile at the same time. Jumping from her bed, she went and hugged her.

"Oh my God! This has been happening for real," an astonished Cyril said, with his eyes wide open.

"Kate … Cyril." Doris sobbed, hugging them both.

"I am so sorry for whatever happened, sweetheart," Kate said, trying to console her.

"We missed you, Doris." Cyril wanted her to feel comfortable too.

Doris saw the book lying on the floor, picked it up without saying anything, and flipped the pages. She could see that it was no longer empty.

"The pages kept filling automatically with all the events that were happening with you in there," Kate explained.

"That is how we knew that you were fine ... until the end." Cyril added.

"Are you all right, Doris?" Kate asked.

"I don't know. I am not sure if this life is real anymore," Doris said, feeling lost.

"You are back, Doris, and we here are real. You are back to your real life, where your family has been going crazy waiting for you," Cyril said, holding her shoulder.

"Then, why do I want to see Edward? This is so embarrassing" Doris said, with a cracked voice, hiding her face in her palms.

"Oh, sweety." Kate hugged her, and Doris started to cry louder.

Kate's mom came to her room, hearing the noise. She was astonished to see Doris.

Doris was in the beach dress she wore before getting lost, with some sand still clinging to her skin.

"Doris, you are alive! Where have you been?" Kate's mom asked with great surprise.

"Mom, will you please leave?" Kate asked.

"No. You need to tell me what happened. You have been missing for months. Your parents put my daughter and Cyril behind bars, accusing them of murdering you. We got them released, as they had no proof against that accusation. I need to know what happened. Are you all right? You look like a mess." Kate's mom wanted to know what had happened and where she had been.

"Not the time, Mom, really." Kate pushed her mom back out the door and closed it.

"I am sorry about my mom. She was also concerned about you," Kate tried to explain.

"You were put behind bars by my parents?" Doris asked, wiping her tears.

"It's not their fault, Doris. It had been quite long, and they started to panic when you didn't return for days. Earlier we were taken only for investigation but then they got us arrested. They thought that we killed you or something," Cyril explained.

"Oh my God! How long have I been in there?" Doris asked.

"It has been seven months, Doris, since you disappeared," Kate answered.

"I can't believe this. Do my parents think I am dead? Your mom thought I was dead." Doris was going crazy.

"Oh no, sweety. Your parents love you so much. Your mom never lost her hope. When she did not see any other way of finding you, she approached us, apologized for putting us behind bars, listened, and understood our part of the story. She used to read this diary too. Every day, we returned this to her at dusk so she could make sure that you were fine. However, we could not convince other people that you were alive. So many still think that we killed you," Kate said.

"I am so sorry, you guys," Doris said.

"Why are you? This was not your fault," Cyril said.

"Yes, you're right. This is all his fault," Doris said, looking at the diary, picking it up, and angrily throwing it outside the window. "You ruined everything, Fitzgerald, and you think I am going to free you? No, I will not, and I will not even let anybody to. You both just rot like that," Doris shouted from the window at the diary lying on the pavement outside.

"It's all right, Doris. Come on. Let's take you back home. Your family is dying to see you again and to know that you are really alive and that we are not crazy people who made up a stupid story," Cyril said.

Kate gave her some clean clothes to wear, and they all left for Doris's place. When they all came out, Doris saw the diary lying on the pavement with its pages opened. Edward's picture was on the opened page. She picked up the book and read the lines below it, which were about the time Edward proposed to her and they spent a beautiful time together.

"Nice try, Fitzgerald. You are quite a sly fox." Doris closed the diary and decided to keep it.

"What are you doing, Doris? You are taking this with you?" Cyril asked.

"I want to read it, Cyril. He's being so clever. If I leave him here, he will surely play with another life. I better keep it with myself. Also, the sweetest memories of my life are on these pages. Although they were all an illusion, to me, they were as real as you both standing here with me right now. Christine, Edward, Cherry …" Doris said, keeping the diary in her bag.

They all then left for her house.

When they reached, it was again so overwhelming for her to see her parents and little brother after so long. Her family cried with joy to see her back.

Sweet Memories

Doris was again back to her real life, but she was a whole new person. She was more responsible, far more mature than she had been earlier, more hardworking, and no more a spoiled brat. Her habit of waking up late changed, and now, she was the first one to wake up at her house—even before the maids they had.

After a long time, Doris woke up on her cozy bed. Yet, she missed the aura of Christine's place, the fragrance of freshly baked bread and muffins, the chirrup of birds, the fresh air. It was not that she did not like being back, but she felt something was missing. She wanted both. Gaining one life at the loss of the other was unacceptable to her. She was overwhelmed by all of this. Disappointed, she got out of bed and looked around her room. The view was a big change. She held the diary and flipped through its pages. She could see a picture in which she and Christine worked together early in the morning in the kitchen and smiled with pain in her eyes. She realized how that girl had unexpectedly changed her to the core. She could never imagine her new self and wasn't sure how people were going to take her.

This sudden realization made her mad at Fitzgerald again, and she threw the diary back at her bed.

The moment she was about to turn back for the door, she could see the pages flipping and a light coming out of the book. Slowly, she moved toward it and held it again, reading the page to which the book opened. It said, "Start anew again with your new self. Make up for your past mistakes, as you know that you are a much better person now. Make up to your family, your friends, and your acquaintances with whom you were unfair, and that will help you. Not everyone gets a chance to fix things like that." It was as if the book could understand what she was thinking.

"Seriously? Look who is giving me moral ideas," Doris taunted the diary. "This can't be Fitzgerald for sure though. It must surely be you, Adyren. Please stop talking to me if that's you. I don't need your help," she continued.

The diary flipped another page with something freshly written: "It is me, Fitzgerald."

"Really? I wanna throw up then," Doris taunted him again, folding her arms.

Fitzgerald wanted Doris to understand his side of the story too. Hence, he did not quit trying to do so in his own way. He communicated again: "I know you will not want to listen to me, and I do not even deserve that. But just know that I have been here so long that I have had enough time to realize how wrong I was and what I did. I know taking you into the story was wrong too, but this was the only way. You have no idea how it was for me to be stuck in here, in this form, for centuries, watching the world go forward. I know I have been wrong in everything, but do I not deserve forgiveness ever? Even after this long?"

Doris didn't say anything and left her room, keeping the diary in a drawer. Even though she hated Fitzgerald, she considered his suggestion. She decided to make up to her family first, by being a better daughter and sister. Since she woke up early in the morning, she did all the household chores before anyone was awake and went to the kitchen to make what she had learned from Christine, as she knew much about it now. She took some gingerbread and fresh juice to her parents and woke them up. It was quite surprising for them indeed.

"Good morning, Mom. Good morning, Dad. Your breakfast is ready," said Doris with a lovely smile.

"Good morning. Where did you get these from, so early in the morning?" Doris's dad asked.

"I made it on my own," Doris replied.

"You did! Really? Oh my God. Look, honey. Can you believe this? Our daughter made these cute gingerbreads," he said to his wife.

"I know." Doris's mom stood up and hugged her daughter. She knew how she had changed and was happy to see her being so responsible and caring.

"Oh, it's delicious too, " Doris's father said, taking a bite of a gingerbread. "I feel like distributing this to everyone and telling them that my own little daughter made this wonderful thing," he continued.

"That's so sweet of you, Dad. I am glad that you like it so much. But trust me, it stands nowhere in front of Christine's—" Doris stopped in the middle of her statement as her parents saw her.

"I am so sorry, Doris. I wish I could help you in some way. I cannot even imagine how it must be for you," Mr. William said, keeping his hand on Doris's shoulder.

"I am fine, Dad. You don't know how strong I have become. I wanted to apologize to both of you for being such a bad kid, making your life so difficult by being the way I was," Doris said.

"Oh, what are you saying, honey? You know that is not true. We love you more than anything, however you are. It is just that I wanted you to be more responsible and a good person, because I did not want bad things to happen to my little daughter. I wanted you to take your studies seriously, because I want you to do well later in your future. Sorry if it came across as me loving you less because that is not true. You have no idea how it has been for us without you. Yeah, sometimes, we used to get mad at you, but which parents don't get mad at their kids? That does not mean that they do not love them. You and George are our treasures. You are back, and that is the most important thing to both of us," Doris's mom said, kissing her forehead.

"I promise that I will be a better and more responsible person from now on, Mom. I love you," Doris said, hugging her mom back.

"I love you too, sweetheart," her mom replied with tears in her eyes.

Doris went to her brother next with breakfast for him too.

"Georgy." Doris tried waking him up.

"I will wake up in five minutes," George said, covering his head with a pillow.

"Wake up, sleepyhead. You won't believe what I did for you," Doris said, snatching his pillow.

"What?" George woke up annoyed but was surprised to find Doris with breakfast for him.

"Look, I made you gingerbread," Doris said with excitement.

"You made it? It is poisoned, isn't it?" George said, taking one in his hand, smelling it, and checking it out strangely.

"No, you idiot. Why would I poison it?" Doris asked.

"Because you hate me. Remember?" George said.

"I don't *hate* you. Who said that?" Doris asked.

"You said it. Did you hit your head hard somewhere? You do not remember anything," George replied.

"I never meant it, you idiot. Moreover, you have no idea how much I missed you all this while. However, you make sense. I know how bad I have been to you. I never realized that the way I treated you could make you think I hated you. But I love you so much. I have always loved you, and I'm really sorry for the way I was before. You are my baby brother. I love you the most. It's just that I always felt you were annoying, but I never realized my life would be a bore without you. You are the first thrill and joy of my life," Doris said, coming close to him and hugging him. "Here, consider this as a token of apology and a promise from my end that I will be the best sister." Doris took one of the gingerbreads and offered it to him.

George took a bite and liked it a lot. He was touched, but surely, he could not show that. "You are apologizing, making such delicious things, speaking emotionally—who are you? And what have you done to my sister?"

"Oh, I locked her in a closet for not being good to you," she replied, tickling him.

"I missed you too," George said.

"I just pray that life makes it up to her," Mr. William said to his wife, standing at the door and watching both of his kids getting along.

It was a good start for Doris. She apologized to her maids when they arrived, and that was a surprise for them too. With the help of her father, she returned to school. Everyone was astonished to find out she was back. So many thought that she was no more, and her teachers and friends did not accept her return. She was a completely different person though. Everyone was of course surprised to see her back but were more surprised to see how different she had become. She was much nicer to her teachers and everyone she encountered, and Doris herself liked changing into a better person. She noticed how the change in her behavior also changed how everyone responded to her, just as Christine used to say in her mirror theory.

The day went quite well. Doris felt happy about how things went but was overwhelmed that she could not share it with Christine or Edward, whom she had gotten so used to. She never thought that she would feel this void left by them. She smiled at the world outside but was so broken on the inside. She had fallen in love with someone who didn't even exist in the real world, and it sucked.

When she returned home, she ran to see Edward's picture in the book, which was the only place where she could see him. She read her story, which was all documented in there, all night and experienced many happy and devastating moments at the same time throughout her story. At the end, she felt anger for Fitzgerald, but it surely made her think about whether he truly deserved to be trapped forever, as written on the last page. He had been trapped inside for about eight to nine hundred years.

It was dawn, and Doris could not sleep because of her thoughts. She wandered around in her balcony with the diary in her hands. Even if she knew that everything in her real life was better now, she was unsure how she would be able to move on. She was deeply in love with a character from a long-past time. She stared at Edward's picture in the book again and ran her fingers through his picture, missing him. She knew that she needed to come out of this, so she closed the diary with tears in her eyes and looked at the stars above. The twinkling stars gradually became dimmer as daylight overtook the sky. The morning breeze was lovely and encouraged her to start anew, as a new start would be far better and full of light, like a new day. It would win over the little light she had from the stars.

She thought that if she did not free him, what happened to her would happen to someone else too, and whoever got trapped again would have to go through what she went through. Doris had a forgiving heart now and decided to release Fitzgerald and Adyren. Hence, she tore the diary with tears in her eyes, shouting, "Fine, you win, Fitzgerald! Go! Go away. You were worthy of this curse, but I think it is enough for you. You are a terrible person for taking people in just to make them release you from there. You can't do that without their will. You just can't. And just because of that, you should not be released. However, I haven't been a good person either. And if this hadn't happened to me, I may not have become the better person I am right now. It pains my heart to admit that I would never have met such wonderful people that I met being in there. I wouldn't have known true care, real help, or unconditional love. It pains the core of my heart, but thank you for letting me know Christine, Cherry, and Edward. And that is why I release you from this curse, knowing what you did, understanding that you have paid enough, and hoping that you realize now that what you did was not right and that it got you nothing but darkness in your own life."

Chapter 27

The Happy Ending

The moment Doris tore the diary, shredded pieces of paper started to collect themselves in the air and soon took the shape of Fitzgerald, still made of gathering paper shreds and floating in the air over her balcony.

"Fitz … Fitzgerald!" Doris trembled, as the figure looked like a ghost, which she wasn't expecting.

"Yes, Doris. It is I, Fitzgerald. I cannot thank you enough for releasing my soul, which was trapped in here for so long. You did so even though what I did to you affected your life so much. I cannot apologize enough for my actions," Fitzgerald said.

"I don't know what to say to you, Fitzgerald. You have changed my life entirely. However, how do I forgive you for playing with my life and emotions? What do I do now?" Doris questioned Fitzgerald.

"Honestly, I don't know. But I am sure you are going to be fine," Fitzgerald replied.

"I am going to be fine? That's what you got! You intentionally made me fall in love with Edward. You intentionally let me get used to having Christine around for everything. And now, you say you don't know?" Doris was expecting something better at least.

"I am sorry about that. I said it because you are one tough girl. Nevertheless, I did not have a choice, you see. I told you that I was trapped in the book for way too long. I had to try escaping somehow. I am really sorry for the approach I took, but that was the only way for me. Nobody would want to stay like that for eternity, knowing that they had some way out—even though it was a tough one." Fitzgerald tried to make her understand why he did what he did.

"You know, you could just have written the story in there for someone to read and decide if you deserved to be released." Doris tried to give him the alternative he should have followed.

"Oh, you think that would have worked and that I never tried that in all the time I had? You tell me, would you have ever cared to read the story written in a decaying diary that you found on a beach? Unless a treasure map is involved, nobody is curious enough to even flip through the pages of such a book. Besides, that was the first thing I followed for years. But trust me, that was the stupidest approach I followed. That wasted more of my time in there. Most of the people back then could not read. A few people did not want to read the story, and a few of them just laughed and threw me back, thinking that it was some joke.

"One of them, I remember, did read it all and took it seriously, but she did not think I deserved to be freed. The next thing I tried was to take people in just to show them what was happening around without letting them be part of the story. But whoever I did this to just ran away the moment they came out. They were too afraid to stay and think about me. Like you, I had taken a man in too, but taking a man in to realize anything was a really bad decision. He started assaulting Christine, seeing her alone. Even though she is fictional inside, I threw him out myself. And then, he threw me into the sea.

"I thought the water in the sea would tear me to shreds or decay me with time and I would perhaps be released. But no, I just floated in the box and reached the shores of America. I waited and waited for about a century to be discovered by you. I was beneath the sands but used to listen to people above. I educated myself about a few new things going on around the world. The new language that people use here, for example—which I used in your time in the book so you could communicate with the people you met. When you found me after such a long time, I could only think of trying my best to escape. I kept you involved throughout because I wanted you to be there until the end. I wanted you to take part in the story, so you would know it all and could experience how it was and how it all happened. So, please do not think that I did not try a simpler approach." Fitzgerald tried to explain his actions.

"Why did you make me fall in love with him? And why the lies? You could have shown me that Christine was with Edward. Why the extra drama of changing the name and involving me so much?" Doris questioned him.

"Like I said, my dear girl, you would not have wanted to stay in there for long in that case. You were not trying to get along with Christine in the beginning but were trying to find a way out. It was only when you started liking Edward that you stopped thinking about leaving. That is why making you fall in love with someone was necessary. Also, it kept you more involved in the main story," Fitzgerald explained again.

"I don't know what to say, but I am still mad at you." Doris could understand him, but her being angry at him did not need a reason.

"I understand that completely. You have every right to be angry. I know you fell in love with him so much, and I am immensely sorry about it. But believe me, Doris, you are a good person—far better than I ever was. Your life will surely make it up to you someday, with everything better. I know this for sure. I have been in this form for centuries, feeling hopeless, but you came as a light in the darkness for me and made possible something I had deemed impossible. So, I know for sure that life will bring light to your life too. You at least have my blessings for that. Even though I was the evil one, I still pray that you get what you are looking for, regardless of how impossible it seems." Fitzgerald gave her his best.

"I forgive you, Fitzgerald. Thank you. I feel much better seeing someone from the story again—even though it is just you. I don't know what to wish for you, but I hope that your soul rests in peace wherever it goes. Goodbye, Fitzgerald," she said, looking at the sky.

A cool breeze touched Doris, and she could hear a whisper saying, "Bless you, my child. Believe in kindness and goodwill, and that will be returned to you. You will find your love and yourself soon."

"Goodbye, Adyren," Doris said, looking around and finding nobody. But she felt Adyren's presence.

A few days passed. Doris started to remain quiet, cutting herself out from her social circles and avoiding her friends. Her parents and friends were indeed happy that she was back but were worried about her emotional breakdowns. They tried their best to make her happy, and Doris appreciated that. But deep inside, she was unable to come back to the present. She tried hard though.

Kate and Cyril had changed too because of what had happened and what their friend went through. They tried not to leave her alone much—even though they were now dating—so Doris would not feel lonely. However, they could not see her this way for long and tried asking her to talk about her feelings so she could feel better.

"You need to stop living this way, Doris. We are sorry about what happened, but you can't do this to yourself. Being like this is not going to help you. This is only going to worsen your health. Look at yourself. We can't see you like this," Kate finally said.

"I am sorry that I am not a fun like before, Kate, but I am not sure I could ever become like that again. I just look back at myself and see how horrible I was. I was not a good person. I started loving it there. I learned kindness and empathy, and I completely understand that you are not liking me now. Also, you and Cyril are dating, and you are always wasting your time being with me when you can rather be together happily. You guys don't have to spoil your fun on my account," Doris said, understanding that her friends might not want to be with her anymore.

"What the hell! You can't say that. We are not that mean, Doris. We are really worried about you. It is not about fun. We have known each other since we were kids. The three of us have cared for each other every time, through evilness or anything else for that matter. Whatever happened to you affected us too. Of course, not as much as you because you were taken alone, but trust me, we both used to read everything about you every time like crazy because we wanted to make sure you were okay.

"Also, don't ever think that you were not a good person before. You were about to sacrifice Edward to Christine, and such a decision, my girl, needs a heart and a strong soul, which you had from the very beginning. This is not something you learned there. It's what you've had from the beginning. Yeah, we were not very nice to people, and we had our fun at their expense, but we never hurt anyone. We were just living our lives on our own terms. And about us, had we been so mean, we would have stopped caring about you. But we never did. We've always cared for you, Doris, and we can't see you like this." Kate spoke her heart out, as she was hurt at what Doris assumed about their feelings.

"God, I am sorry, Kate. I don't know why I said that. It's just that this was the reason I did not consider loving anybody because I was afraid it would hurt. I always hid it from you both, but I was always capable of loving someone. I just was not capable of losing him. And that is why I have always been such a pain to everybody—because I knew things don't last long in real life. I feared this since the beginning, and look, I am facing it now." Doris finally spoke about the innermost feelings she had always held about love.

"Oh, Doris, you think we never knew that? You are facing your fear remarkably. However, you don't have to be sad all the time. Just try to divert your mind and let us help you with that. We both care about you so much. And when you are sad, it makes us sad too," Kate said, holding her shoulders.

"I never knew that you cared about me this much!" Doris hugged her.

"Oh, and you thought that Christine loved you more than us?" Kate said, teasing her.

"I don't know," Doris replied.

"That is why I have been so jealous of that Christine girl," Kate said, winking at her.

"What, really?" Doris said, smiling.

"Why not? You are only mine, babe. No one can dare take you from me. If that wasn't just a damn diary, I would have shown her when she tried stealing you from me here," Kate teased her.

"Don't worry, Kate. You have always been my first love." Doris winked. They always spoke to each other this way out of friendship.

"Hey, what about me?" Cyril asked.

"Oh, you are just a stand-in, Cyril," Kate teased him.

"You girls ... get a room!" Cyril said, and they all laughed.

One fine morning, Kate and Cyril stopped at Doris's house to pick her up for school, as they did every day lately. With their silly jokes and efforts to lighten Doris's mood, they reached the school. At the same time, another car stopped right next to theirs. When Doris came out, she stumbled but luckily fell into the arms of someone. It was a man who alighted from the car beside theirs. But that was not all. He surprised Doris to her core, as she knew that face very well. Her hands automatically ran to touch his face in disbelief, and her lips could not help themselves from saying, "Edward ... my Edward?"

It was a man who looked exactly like Edward.

Anyway, the man was astonished as well, as he had never met this girl in his life before. But she knew his name. Also, like the Edward in the story, he fell for her beauty and the way she looked at him. He kept staring at her and her eyes, which were filled with joyous tears, looking at him after so long. She stood up and hugged him tight, saying, "Oh, don't leave me ever again, or I will die. I love you. I love you so so much."

Edward could feel her deep love, and he was touched by her very much and felt the best ever hugging her. He was definitely confused though. However, he could feel some strong connection and didn't step back. Instead, he just held her tighter.

Kate and Cyril were watching all of this, side hugging each other with tears in their eyes but also smiled spanning across their faces, as they knew what was happening.

Finally, Fitzgerald's blessings and Adyren's magical words came true. She got what she was praying hard for—her love, Edward.

Life is not so harsh that it would let anyone live with the sacrifice that they made. It indeed rewards you with something far better if that sacrifice is made wholeheartedly for someone's good.

---------- *The End* ----------

www.ingramcontent.com/pod-product-compliance
Lightning Source LLC
LaVergne TN
LVHW041219080526
838199LV00082B/971